YOUR TIME FREEDOM

PRODUCTIVITY JOURNAL

A daily guide to focus on what matters until it's done

NAME: ....

ADDRESS: ....

PHONE: ....

START DATE: ....

CREATED BY

evolution
BUSINESS CONSULTING

"It's not how early you wake up, or how late you stay up. It's what you're doing with your time when you're up."

JAVIER LORIE

ACKNOWLEDGEMENTS

There are two books that helped me when creating the "90 Day Time Freedom Planner".

The "Seven Habits of Highly Effective People" by Stephen R. Covey helped me develop the foundations to effectively manage my time.

And the "Finisher Journal" by Javier Lorie. This book inspired me to share how I plan and execute my days so I can be more effective than many of my contemporaries.

DEDICATION

Without the opportunity to own a business I
would not have learnt the lessons I have, for this
I thank my Father.

Without the desire for improvement I would not
have looked for a better way, for this I thank my
Mother.

Without the support of my wife, Shannon, nothing
would be possible.

Without my two children, my head would get too
big and explode, they keep me grounded!

ABOUT THE AUTHOR

I believe that every high performer needs a coach, whether it's an elite athlete, an employee, or a business owner.

I have had mentors and coaches. Some of them have been my direct supervisors, others have been a senior person in the organisation.

When I moved to owning my business, I sought out independent Business Coaches. I am who I am today because of their influence and teachings.

In 2006, I became part owner and Managing Director of our family owned company, Fire & Emergency Services SA. Since then I have more than quadrupled the company's revenue in a slow and price sensitive market. Along the way, I have made mistakes and learnt from them, enabling the business to grow into one of the leading companies in our class – and we have awards to prove it!

Since 2012, I have taken what I have learnt as a business owner and given back; running business coaching programs with start-ups, growing companies, and business owners trying to regain control of their lives.

Too often I have witnessed how a business owner's life has been ruined by their business.

I don't want that to happen to you.

I believe that business owners deserve to have the work life balance that was expected (and hoped for) when they started their business.

I want to help you in this constant struggle.

Alan Short

"Time is the coin of your life.

It is the only coin you have, and only you can determine how it will be spent.

Be careful lest you let other people spend it for you."

CARL SANDBURG

HOW TO USE

Time is the one currency that you cannot grow.

Everybody (no matter their age, experience, or wealth) has just 24 hours in each day and 7 days in each week. You can't save your hours or days and use them later. Once time has passed, it's gone forever.

So, how are you using your time? Are you spending it effectively?

Using time effectively is very different from using time efficiently. Being efficient means that you are getting the most output from your time.

Being effective is using your time to get more of the important work done, for your business, your community and yourself.

In my book "Time Freedom: how to work 10 hours less in just 60 days" I introduce the tools to make sure you use your time effectively to support the lifestyle you want.

Often business owners and leaders are so focused on their work that they lose connection with their family, their friends, and their health. I call this being enslaved to your business or job.

Your Planner and the "Time Freedom" book are designed to work together to help you build the lifestyle you dream of.

Or, what I call achieving Time Freedom!

If you don't have a copy of the book, visit **evolutionbusiness.com.au** and get your copy today.

"A dream written down with
a date becomes a goal.

A goal broken down into steps
becomes a plan.

A plan backed by action makes
your dreams come true."

GREG REID

HOW TO USE

Your Planner has three key parts:

1. Defining your 90 day goals

2. Defining your weekly priorities

3. Daily planning

Let's explore these in detail.

1 | DEFINING YOUR 90 DAY GOALS

90 day goals allow you enough time to take definitive action, but not too long that they are too abstract.

How many goals do you have?

As ambitious people we often have a lot of goals that we want to achieve, this book only allows you to have up to three goals.

Why so few? We have a tendency to overestimate what we can do in the short term, and underestimate what we can do in the long term. So, let's start small, if you achieve one, two or three goals within 90 days then celebrate and rest, or pick another goal knowing that you are ahead of your plan.

In an ideal world your 90 day goals will be based on a yearly planning process. If you are interested in getting help to undertake a longer-term plan, contact us at **alan.short@evolutionbusiness.com.au** or visit our website **evolutionbusiness.com.au** to book a call.

At the end of 90 days you will review how you went and what you have learnt, so that you can be better set up for success for the next 90 days.

2 | DEFINING YOUR WEEKLY PRIORITIES

Often our life and work distract us from our goals, so each week we need to reorientate ourself to our goals.

At the start of every week you will reaffirm your goals by writing them down. This activates your reticular activation system towards achieving these goals. In other words, by frequently keeping your goals in front of you they will stay in your consciousness, and you will find opportunities to achieve your goals everywhere.

After your goals are written down, you then list the main tasks you want to achieve AND give them a priority.

A | IMPORTANT AND URGENT
The one, two, or three things that you must get done this week.

B | IMPORTANT FOR YOU TO GET DONE
These are often what you need to get done to achieve your 90 day goals.

C | URGENT TASKS
These are tasks that you need to get done. And while They might be important to others, they are not critical for you.

D | EVERYTHING ELSE
And be honest, do you really need to do these items?

For more information on setting priorities refer to section 6 of my "Time Freedom" book.

You need to be realistic with how much time you really have.

In your Planner map out all the meetings and boundaries that you have in your workday. The space around this time is all that you can use each day to complete your weekly priorities. Do you have time to achieve them? If not then move them to next week!

For more information on setting boundaries to your working day refer to section 5 of my book "Time Freedom".

At the end of each week, you will review how you went - how far did you progress towards your 90 day goals?

WHAT IS WORKING?
Which completed tasks should you focus more time on?

WHAT ISN'T WORKING?
What tasks didn't work as well as you hoped? They might need to be fixed, improved or removed.

• WHAT DID YOU LEARN?
Take a minute to think about what the biggest takeaway or lesson you learnt from the week was.

3 | DEFINING YOUR DAILY TASKS

One of the biggest mistakes we make when planning our day is to start with a single list of all the things that we need to do.

Each day you cross off a few items and add a few items... and feel like you are not moving ahead, in fact, you often feel like you are going backwards.

Having a central list is important, but it is not part of your daily plan.

The first step is to block out the meetings you have, and the boundaries to your working day in the timeline on the left-hand page.

Next add blocks of time for travel, breaks, and repetitive activities that happen every day, like reviewing emails or returning phone messages after a meeting.

Now you can see the time that you have available to complete your tasks. Some days you will have no time available, on those days you won't list any tasks on the page.

If you have time available, make a list on the left hand page of the tasks that you plan to get done.

Remember to think about how long the task will take, if you only have 1 hour and the task will take 4 hours to complete then don't list it, either list a smaller part/sub task of the larger task or realise that it won't get done and select another task.

During the day you will be able to celebrate your success by ticking off each meeting you have and marking off each task you complete.

You can do this all in one colour, but I recommend that you engage the visual part of your brain by using multiple colours.

I recommend:

BLACK
to block out your meetings in your time line

BLUE
to list the tasks and when you expect to complete them

GREEN
to tick off items and mark tasks as complete

RED
to show where you have been unable to complete a task. Either delete the task as it's no longer required or move it into another day

There is nothing more satisfying to reflect on a day with green marks showing that you achieved everything you had planned.

OUTCOME GOALS

Narrow your focus to one specific and measurable goal that you can accomplish in the next 90 days.

PRIMARY GOAL

Write down your primary goal using the format "I will X from Y to Z by When."

e.g : "Increase profits from $10k to $20k by April 1"

I will ....

.... **by** ....

90 days from today

SECONDARY GOAL

It is highly recommended that you put all your effort and attention into achieving your primary goal. Your secondary goal should only be set after your primary goal has been met.

I will ....

.... **by** ....

90 days from today

TERTIARY GOAL

Your tertiary goal comes after your secondary goal has been met.

I will ....

.... **by** ....

90 days from today

KEY MOTIVATIONS

Write down the three motivations you have for achieving these goals.

1. ....

2. ....

3. ....

ACTION PLAN

"A goal without a plan is just a wish". Having determined your goals, it's time to formulate a strategy to reach them.

PRIMARY GOAL NEXT STEPS

1. ....

2. ....

3. ....

SECONDARY GOAL NEXT STEPS

1. ....

2. ....

3. ....

TERTIARY GOAL NEXT STEPS

1. ....

2. ....

3. ....

ACCOUNTABILITY

How will you stay committed to achieving your goal?

1. ....

2. ....

3. ....

WEEK 1 COMMITMENT

WEEKS LEFT IN QUARTER

`13` `12` `11` `10` `9` `8` `7` `6` `5` `4` `3` `2` `1`

Restate your goals each week to maintain your focus

PRIMARY GOAL

. . . .

SECONDARY GOAL

. . . .

TERTIARY GOAL

. . . .

MUST-DELIVER TASK

What is the most relevant milestone in your Action Plan at the moment?
Towards achieving this milestone, what is the most important task you must finish this week?

☐ . . . . **A***

SECONDARY TASKS

List and prioritise secondary tasks using:

A = Must do this week

B = Good to do this week

C = Can do next week

☐ . . . .

☐ . . . .

☐ . . . .

☐ . . . .

☐ . . . .

☐ . . . .

Keep track of the progress you make on every task using these symbols:

☑ In Progress   ☑ Completed   ☒ Deleted   ⇨ Deferred

AFTER-ACTION REVIEW

Review your results after completing your work week by answering the following questions:

HOW FAR DID YOU GET?

Evaluate your progress and visualise it using the progress bars.

PRIMARY GOAL	20%	40%	60%	80%
SECONDARY GOAL	20%	40%	60%	80%
TERTIARY GOAL	20%	40%	60%	80%

☐ In Progress   ☐ Completed

WHAT IS WORKING?

List the activities you've completed in the past few weeks that you should focus on more.

1. ....

2. ....

3. ....

WHAT DIDN'T WORK?

List the activities that need to be fixed, improved, or removed.

1. ....

2. ....

3. ....

WHAT DID YOU LEARN?

Take a minute to reflect on the biggest takeaway from this week.

....

WEEK 1

MONDAY	TUESDAY	WEDNESDAY
7		
8		
9		
10		
11		
12		
1		
2		
3		
4		
5		
6		
7		

THURSDAY	FRIDAY	SAT	SUN
7			
8			
9			
10			
11			
12			
1			
2			
3			
4			
5			
6			
7			

MONDAY   /   /

MOST IMPORTANT TASK

What can you accomplish today to meet your
weekly objective?

☐ ....

....

SECONDARY TASK

These tasks can only be done after you've
completed your MIT

☐ ....

☐ ....

ADDITIONAL TASKS & REMINDERS

List additional tasks and reminders for the day.

☐ ....

☐ ....

☐ ....

☐ ....

☐ ....

☐ ....

☑ In Progress	☒ Completed
☒ Deleted	⇨ Deferred

6 ————————————

7 ------------------------

8 ------------------------

9 ------------------------

10 ------------------------

11 ------------------------

12 ------------------------

1 ------------------------

2 ------------------------

3 ------------------------

4 ------------------------

5 ------------------------

6 ------------------------

7 ------------------------

NOTES / IDEAS

Write down any notes or ideas you have today. For future reference, index them on page 5.

....
....
....
....
....
....
....
....
....
....
....
....
....
....
....
....
....
....
....
....
....
....
....
....
....
....
....
....
....
....
....

TUESDAY   /   /

MOST IMPORTANT TASK

What can you accomplish today to meet your
weekly objective?

☐ ....

SECONDARY TASK

These tasks can only be done after you've
completed your MIT

☐ ....

☐ ....

ADDITIONAL TASKS & REMINDERS

List additional tasks and reminders for the day.

☐ ....

☐ ....

☐ ....

☐ ....

☐ ....

☐ ....

	In Progress		Completed
	Deleted		Deferred

6 ——————————————

7 ——————————————

8 ——————————————

9 ——————————————

10 ——————————————

11 ——————————————

12 ——————————————

1 ——————————————

2 ——————————————

3 ——————————————

4 ——————————————

5 ——————————————

6 ——————————————

7 ——————————————

NOTES / IDEAS

Write down any notes or ideas you have today. For future reference, index them on page 5.

WEDNESDAY   /   /

MOST IMPORTANT TASK

What can you accomplish today to meet your weekly objective?

☐ ....

....

SECONDARY TASK

These tasks can only be done after you've completed your MIT

☐ ....

☐ ....

ADDITIONAL TASKS & REMINDERS

List additional tasks and reminders for the day.

☐ ....

☐ ....

☐ ....

☐ ....

☐ ....

☐ ....

▧ In Progress   ▩ Completed

☒ Deleted   ⇨ Deferred

6 ————————————————
....
7 ————————————————
....
8 ————————————————
....
9 ————————————————
....
10 ————————————————
....
11 ————————————————
....
12 ————————————————
....
1 ————————————————
....
2 ————————————————
....
3 ————————————————
....
4 ————————————————
....
5 ————————————————
....
6 ————————————————
....
7 ————————————————

NOTES / IDEAS

Write down any notes or ideas you have today. For future reference, index them on page 5.

THURSDAY / /

MOST IMPORTANT TASK

What can you accomplish today to meet your
weekly objective?

- [ ] ....

....

SECONDARY TASK

These tasks can only be done after you've
completed your MIT

- [ ] ....
- [ ] ....

ADDITIONAL TASKS & REMINDERS

List additional tasks and reminders for the day.

- [ ] ....
- [ ] ....
- [ ] ....
- [ ] ....
- [ ] ....
- [ ] ....

In Progress   Completed

Deleted   Deferred

6 ——————————

7 ——————————

8 ——————————

9 ——————————

10 ——————————

11 ——————————

12 ——————————

1 ——————————

2 ——————————

3 ——————————

4 ——————————

5 ——————————

6 ——————————

7 ——————————

NOTES / IDEAS

Write down any notes or ideas you have today. For future reference, index them on page 5.

FRIDAY   /   /

MOST IMPORTANT TASK

What can you accomplish today to meet your
weekly objective?

SECONDARY TASK

These tasks can only be done after you've
completed your MIT

ADDITIONAL TASKS & REMINDERS

List additional tasks and reminders for the day.

	In Progress		Completed
	Deleted		Deferred

6

7

8

9

10

11

12

1

2

3

4

5

6

7

NOTES / IDEAS

Write down any notes or ideas you have today. For future reference, index them on page 5.

SATURDAY   /   /

MOST IMPORTANT TASK

What can you accomplish today to meet your
weekly objective?

☐ ....

SECONDARY TASK

These tasks can only be done after you've
completed your MIT

☐ ....

☐ ....

ADDITIONAL TASKS & REMINDERS

List additional tasks and reminders for the day.

☐ ....

☐ ....

☐ ....

☐ ....

☐ ....

☐ ....

In Progress	Completed
Deleted	Deferred

6 ————————————

7 ————————————

8 ————————————

9 ————————————

10 ————————————

11 ————————————

12 ————————————

1 ————————————

2 ————————————

3 ————————————

4 ————————————

5 ————————————

6 ————————————

7 ————————————

NOTES / IDEAS

Write down any notes or ideas you have today. For future reference, index them on page 5.

SUNDAY   /   /

MOST IMPORTANT TASK
What can you accomplish today to meet your
weekly objective?

☐ ....

SECONDARY TASK
These tasks can only be done after you've
completed your MIT

☐ ....

☐ ....

ADDITIONAL TASKS & REMINDERS
List additional tasks and reminders for the day.

☐ ....

☐ ....

☐ ....

☐ ....

☐ ....

☐ ....

▨ In Progress	▦ Completed
☒ Deleted	⇨ Deferred

6 ——————————————

7 ——————————————

8 ——————————————

9 ——————————————

10 ——————————————

11 ——————————————

12 ——————————————

1 ——————————————

2 ——————————————

3 ——————————————

4 ——————————————

5 ——————————————

6 ——————————————

7 ——————————————

NOTES / IDEAS

Write down any notes or ideas you have today. For future reference, index them on page 5.

....
....
....
....
....
....
....
....
....
....
....
....
....
....
....
....
....
....
....
....
....
....
....
....
....
....

WEEK 2 COMMITMENT

WEEKS LEFT IN QUARTER

`13` `12` `11` `10` `9` `8` `7` `6` `5` `4` `3` `2` `1`

Restate your goals each week to maintain your focus

PRIMARY GOAL

....

SECONDARY GOAL

....

TERTIARY GOAL

....

MUST-DELIVER TASK

What is the most relevant milestone in your Action Plan at the moment?
Towards achieving this milestone, what is the most important task you must finish this week?

☐ .... **A***

SECONDARY TASKS

List and prioritise secondary tasks using:

A = Must do this week

B = Good to do this week

C = Can do next week

☐ ....

☐ ....

☐ ....

☐ ....

☐ ....

☐ ....

Keep track of the progress you make on every task using these symbols:

▨ In Progress　　▨ Completed　　☒ Deleted　　⇨ Deferred

AFTER-ACTION REVIEW

Review your results after completing your work week by answering the following questions:

HOW FAR DID YOU GET?
Evaluate your progress and visualise it using the progress bars.

PRIMARY GOAL	20%	40%	60%	80%
SECONDARY GOAL	20%	40%	60%	80%
TERTIARY GOAL	20%	40%	60%	80%

⬚ In Progress   ⬚ Completed

WHAT IS WORKING?
List the activities you've completed in the past few weeks that you should focus on more.

1. ....

2. ....

3. ....

WHAT DIDN'T WORK?
List the activities that need to be fixed, improved, or removed.

1. ....

2. ....

3. ....

WHAT DID YOU LEARN?
Take a minute to reflect on the biggest takeaway from this week.

....

WEEK 2

MONDAY	TUESDAY	WEDNESDAY
7		
8		
9		
10		
11		
12		
1		
2		
3		
4		
5		
6		
7		

THURSDAY	FRIDAY	SAT	SUN
7			
8			
9			
10			
11			
12			
1			
2			
3			
4			
5			
6			
7			

MONDAY / /

Schedule blocks of time to complete your tasks and reminders

MOST IMPORTANT TASK

What can you accomplish today to meet your weekly objective?

☐ ....

....

SECONDARY TASK

These tasks can only be done after you've completed your MIT

☐ ....

☐ ....

ADDITIONAL TASKS & REMINDERS

List additional tasks and reminders for the day.

☐ ....

☐ ....

☐ ....

☐ ....

☐ ....

☐ ....

In Progress   Completed

Deleted   Deferred

6 ————————————

7 ————————————

8 ————————————

9 ————————————

10 ————————————

11 ————————————

12 ————————————

1 ————————————

2 ————————————

3 ————————————

4 ————————————

5 ————————————

6 ————————————

7 ————————————

NOTES / IDEAS

Write down any notes or ideas you have today. For future reference, index them on page 5.

TUESDAY   /   /

MOST IMPORTANT TASK
What can you accomplish today to meet your
weekly objective?

☐ ....

....

SECONDARY TASK
These tasks can only be done after you've
completed your MIT

☐ ....

☐ ....

ADDITIONAL TASKS & REMINDERS
List additional tasks and reminders for the day.

☐ ....

☐ ....

☐ ....

☐ ....

☐ ....

☐ ....

☑ In Progress   ▦ Completed

☒ Deleted   ⇨ Deferred

6 ——————————————————

7 ------------------------------

8 ------------------------------

9 ------------------------------

10 ------------------------------

11 ------------------------------

12 ------------------------------

1 ------------------------------

2 ------------------------------

3 ------------------------------

4 ------------------------------

5 ------------------------------

6 ------------------------------

7 ------------------------------

NOTES / IDEAS

Write down any notes or ideas you have today. For future reference, index them on page 5.

WEDNESDAY / /

MOST IMPORTANT TASK
What can you accomplish today to meet your
weekly objective?

☐ ....

....

SECONDARY TASK
These tasks can only be done after you've
completed your MIT

☐ ....

☐ ....

ADDITIONAL TASKS & REMINDERS
List additional tasks and reminders for the day.

☐ ....

☐ ....

☐ ....

☐ ....

☐ ....

☐ ....

In Progress   Completed

Deleted   Deferred

6 ──────────────

7 ──────────────

8 ──────────────

9 ──────────────

10 ──────────────

11 ──────────────

12 ──────────────

1 ──────────────

2 ──────────────

3 ──────────────

4 ──────────────

5 ──────────────

6 ──────────────

7 ──────────────

NOTES / IDEAS

Write down any notes or ideas you have today. For future reference, index them on page 5.

THURSDAY / /

MOST IMPORTANT TASK
What can you accomplish today to meet your
weekly objective?

SECONDARY TASK
These tasks can only be done after you've
completed your MIT

ADDITIONAL TASKS & REMINDERS
List additional tasks and reminders for the day.

In Progress   Completed

Deleted   Deferred

6

7

8

9

10

11

12

1

2

3

4

5

6

7

NOTES / IDEAS

Write down any notes or ideas you have today. For future reference, index them on page 5.

FRIDAY   /   /

MOST IMPORTANT TASK

What can you accomplish today to meet your
weekly objective?

☐ ....

SECONDARY TASK

These tasks can only be done after you've
completed your MIT

☐ ....

☐ ....

ADDITIONAL TASKS & REMINDERS

List additional tasks and reminders for the day.

☐ ....

☐ ....

☐ ....

☐ ....

☐ ....

☐ ....

	In Progress		Completed
	Deleted		Deferred

6 ——————————————

7 ---------------------------------

8 ---------------------------------

9 ---------------------------------

10 ---------------------------------

11 ---------------------------------

12 ---------------------------------

1 ---------------------------------

2 ---------------------------------

3 ---------------------------------

4 ---------------------------------

5 ---------------------------------

6 ---------------------------------

7 ---------------------------------

NOTES / IDEAS

Write down any notes or ideas you have today. For future reference, index them on page 5.

SATURDAY / /

MOST IMPORTANT TASK

What can you accomplish today to meet your
weekly objective?

☐ ....

....

SECONDARY TASK

These tasks can only be done after you've
completed your MIT

☐ ....

☐ ....

ADDITIONAL TASKS & REMINDERS

List additional tasks and reminders for the day.

☐ ....

☐ ....

☐ ....

☐ ....

☐ ....

☐ ....

◪ In Progress   ▨ Completed

⊠ Deleted   ⇨ Deferred

6 ─────────────────────

7 ─────────────────────

8 ─────────────────────

9 ─────────────────────

10 ─────────────────────

11 ─────────────────────

12 ─────────────────────

1 ─────────────────────

2 ─────────────────────

3 ─────────────────────

4 ─────────────────────

5 ─────────────────────

6 ─────────────────────

7 ─────────────────────

NOTES / IDEAS

Write down any notes or ideas you have today. For future reference, index them on page 5.

SUNDAY   /   /

MOST IMPORTANT TASK

What can you accomplish today to meet your weekly objective?

SECONDARY TASK

These tasks can only be done after you've completed your MIT

ADDITIONAL TASKS & REMINDERS

List additional tasks and reminders for the day.

In Progress   Completed

Deleted   Deferred

6

7

8

9

10

11

12

1

2

3

4

5

6

7

NOTES / IDEAS

Write down any notes or ideas you have today. For future reference, index them on page 5.

WEEK 3 COMMITMENT

WEEKS LEFT IN QUARTER

`13` `12` `11` `10` `9` `8` `7` `6` `5` `4` `3` `2` `1`

Restate your goals each week to maintain your focus

PRIMARY GOAL

....

SECONDARY GOAL

....

TERTIARY GOAL

....

MUST-DELIVER TASK

What is the most relevant milestone in your Action Plan at the moment?
Towards achieving this milestone, what is the most important task you must finish this week?

☐ .... **A***

SECONDARY TASKS

List and prioritise secondary tasks using:

A = Must do this week

B = Good to do this week

C = Can do next week

☐ ....

☐ ....

☐ ....

☐ ....

☐ ....

☐ ....

Keep track of the progress you make on every task using these symbols:

⬚ In Progress ◼ Completed ⊠ Deleted ⇨ Deferred

AFTER-ACTION REVIEW

Review your results after completing your work week by answering the following questions:

HOW FAR DID YOU GET?

Evaluate your progress and visualise it using the progress bars.

	20%	40%	60%	80%	
PRIMARY GOAL	20%	40%	60%	80%	
SECONDARY GOAL	20%	40%	60%	80%	
TERTIARY GOAL	20%	40%	60%	80%	

☐ In Progress   ☐ Completed

WHAT IS WORKING?

List the activities you've completed in the past few weeks that you should focus on more.

1. ....

2. ....

3. ....

WHAT DIDN'T WORK?

List the activities that need to be fixed, improved, or removed.

1. ....

2. ....

3. ....

WHAT DID YOU LEARN?

Take a minute to reflect on the biggest takeaway from this week.

....

WEEK 3

MONDAY	TUESDAY	WEDNESDAY
7		
8		
9		
10		
11		
12		
1		
2		
3		
4		
5		
6		
7		

THURSDAY	FRIDAY	SAT	SUN
7			
8			
9			
10			
11			
12			
1			
2			
3			
4			
5			
6			
7			

MONDAY   / /

MOST IMPORTANT TASK
What can you accomplish today to meet your
weekly objective?

☐ ....

....

SECONDARY TASK
These tasks can only be done after you've
completed your MIT

☐ ....

☐ ....

ADDITIONAL TASKS & REMINDERS
List additional tasks and reminders for the day.

☐ ....

☐ ....

☐ ....

☐ ....

☐ ....

☐ ....

☑ In Progress   ☒ Completed

☒ Deleted   ☐⇨ Deferred

6 ————————————————

7 ------------------------------

8 ------------------------------

9 ------------------------------

10 ------------------------------

11 ------------------------------

12 ------------------------------

1 ------------------------------

2 ------------------------------

3 ------------------------------

4 ------------------------------

5 ------------------------------

6 ------------------------------

7 ------------------------------

NOTES / IDEAS

Write down any notes or ideas you have today. For future reference, index them on page 5.

TUESDAY / /

MOST IMPORTANT TASK

What can you accomplish today to meet your
weekly objective?

- [ ] ....

....

SECONDARY TASK

These tasks can only be done after you've
completed your MIT

- [ ] ....
- [ ] ....

ADDITIONAL TASKS & REMINDERS

List additional tasks and reminders for the day.

- [ ] ....
- [ ] ....
- [ ] ....
- [ ] ....
- [ ] ....
- [ ] ....

◨ In Progress	▦ Completed
⊠ Deleted	⇨ Deferred

6 ———————————————

7 ———————————————

8 ———————————————

9 ———————————————

10 ———————————————

11 ———————————————

12 ———————————————

1 ———————————————

2 ———————————————

3 ———————————————

4 ———————————————

5 ———————————————

6 ———————————————

7 ———————————————

NOTES / IDEAS

Write down any notes or ideas you have today. For future reference, index them on page 5.

WEDNESDAY / /

MOST IMPORTANT TASK

What can you accomplish today to meet your weekly objective?

☐ ....

....

SECONDARY TASK

These tasks can only be done after you've completed your MIT

☐ ....

☐ ....

ADDITIONAL TASKS & REMINDERS

List additional tasks and reminders for the day.

☐ ....

☐ ....

☐ ....

☐ ....

☐ ....

☐ ....

◨ In Progress　　◼ Completed

☒ Deleted　　⇨ Deferred

6 ——————————————

7 --------------------------

8 --------------------------

9 --------------------------

10 --------------------------

11 --------------------------

12 --------------------------

1 --------------------------

2 --------------------------

3 --------------------------

4 --------------------------

5 --------------------------

6 --------------------------

7 --------------------------

NOTES / IDEAS

Write down any notes or ideas you have today. For future reference, index them on page 5.

THURSDAY / /

MOST IMPORTANT TASK
What can you accomplish today to meet your
weekly objective?

☐ ....

SECONDARY TASK
These tasks can only be done after you've
completed your MIT

☐ ....

☐ ....

ADDITIONAL TASKS & REMINDERS
List additional tasks and reminders for the day.

☐ ....

☐ ....

☐ ....

☐ ....

☐ ....

☐ ....

▧ In Progress	▨ Completed
⊠ Deleted	⇨ Deferred

6 ——————————

7 ——————————

8 ——————————

9 ——————————

10 ——————————

11 ——————————

12 ——————————

1 ——————————

2 ——————————

3 ——————————

4 ——————————

5 ——————————

6 ——————————

7 ——————————

NOTES / IDEAS

Write down any notes or ideas you have today. For future reference, index them on page 5.

FRIDAY   /   /

MOST IMPORTANT TASK

What can you accomplish today to meet your
weekly objective?

☐ ....

....

SECONDARY TASK

These tasks can only be done after you've
completed your MIT

☐ ....

☐ ....

ADDITIONAL TASKS & REMINDERS

List additional tasks and reminders for the day.

☐ ....

☐ ....

☐ ....

☐ ....

☐ ....

☐ ....

▨ In Progress   ▨ Completed

☒ Deleted   ⇨ Deferred

6 ——————————————

7 ——————————————

8 ——————————————

9 ——————————————

10 ——————————————

11 ——————————————

12 ——————————————

1 ——————————————

2 ——————————————

3 ——————————————

4 ——————————————

5 ——————————————

6 ——————————————

7 ——————————————

NOTES / IDEAS

Write down any notes or ideas you have today. For future reference, index them on page 5.

SATURDAY / /

Schedule blocks of time to complete your tasks and reminders

MOST IMPORTANT TASK

What can you accomplish today to meet your weekly objective?

SECONDARY TASK

These tasks can only be done after you've completed your MIT

ADDITIONAL TASKS & REMINDERS

List additional tasks and reminders for the day.

In Progress   Completed

Deleted   Deferred

6

7

8

9

10

11

12

1

2

3

4

5

6

7

NOTES / IDEAS

Write down any notes or ideas you have today. For future reference, index them on page 5.

SUNDAY   /   /

Schedule blocks of time to complete your tasks and reminders

MOST IMPORTANT TASK
What can you accomplish today to meet your weekly objective?

☐ --

SECONDARY TASK
These tasks can only be done after you've completed your MIT

☐ --

☐ --

ADDITIONAL TASKS & REMINDERS
List additional tasks and reminders for the day.

☐ --

☐ --

☐ --

☐ --

☐ --

☐ --

▨ In Progress   ▨ Completed
☒ Deleted   ⇨ Deferred

6

7

8

9

10

11

12

1

2

3

4

5

6

7

NOTES / IDEAS

Write down any notes or ideas you have today. For future reference, index them on page 5.

WEEK 4 COMMITMENT

`13` `12` `11` `10` `9` `8` `7` `6` `5` `4` `3` `2` `1`

Restate your goals each week to maintain your focus

PRIMARY GOAL

....

SECONDARY GOAL

....

TERTIARY GOAL

....

MUST-DELIVER TASK

What is the most relevant milestone in your Action Plan at the moment?
Towards achieving this milestone, what is the most important task you must finish this week?

☐ .... **A***

SECONDARY TASKS

List and prioritise secondary tasks using:

A = Must do this week

B = Good to do this week

C = Can do next week

☐ .... |

☐ .... |

☐ .... |

☐ .... |

☐ .... |

☐ .... |

Keep track of the progress you make on every task using these symbols:

☐ In Progress   ☐ Completed   ☒ Deleted   ☐➡ Deferred

AFTER-ACTION REVIEW

Review your results after completing your work week by answering the following questions:

HOW FAR DID YOU GET?

Evaluate your progress and visualise it using the progress bars.

PRIMARY GOAL	20%	40%	60%	80%
SECONDARY GOAL	20%	40%	60%	80%
TERTIARY GOAL	20%	40%	60%	80%

☐ In Progress   ☐ Completed

WHAT IS WORKING?

List the activities you've completed in the past few weeks that you should focus on more.

1. _____

2. _____

3. _____

WHAT DIDN'T WORK?

List the activities that need to be fixed, improved, or removed.

1. _____

2. _____

3. _____

WHAT DID YOU LEARN?

Take a minute to reflect on the biggest takeaway from this week.

_____

WEEK 4

MONDAY	TUESDAY	WEDNESDAY
7		
8		
9		
10		
11		
12		
1		
2		
3		
4		
5		
6		
7		

THURSDAY	FRIDAY	SAT	SUN
7			
8			
9			
10			
11			
12			
1			
2			
3			
4			
5			
6			
7			

MONDAY / /

MOST IMPORTANT TASK

What can you accomplish today to meet your
weekly objective?

SECONDARY TASK

These tasks can only be done after you've
completed your MIT

ADDITIONAL TASKS & REMINDERS

List additional tasks and reminders for the day.

In Progress   Completed

Deleted   Deferred

6

7

8

9

10

11

12

1

2

3

4

5

6

7

NOTES / IDEAS

Write down any notes or ideas you have today. For future reference, index them on page 5.

TUESDAY   /   /

MOST IMPORTANT TASK

What can you accomplish today to meet your
weekly objective?

☐ ....

....

SECONDARY TASK

These tasks can only be done after you've
completed your MIT

☐ ....

☐ ....

ADDITIONAL TASKS & REMINDERS

List additional tasks and reminders for the day.

☐ ....

☐ ....

☐ ....

☐ ....

☐ ....

☐ ....

▨ In Progress	▨ Completed
⊠ Deleted	⇨ Deferred

6 ——————————————

7 ——————————————

8 ——————————————

9 ——————————————

10 ——————————————

11 ——————————————

12 ——————————————

1 ——————————————

2 ——————————————

3 ——————————————

4 ——————————————

5 ——————————————

6 ——————————————

7 ——————————————

NOTES / IDEAS

Write down any notes or ideas you have today. For future reference, index them on page 5.

WEDNESDAY   /   /

MOST IMPORTANT TASK

What can you accomplish today to meet your
weekly objective?

☐ ....

....

SECONDARY TASK

These tasks can only be done after you've
completed your MIT

☐ ....

☐ ....

ADDITIONAL TASKS & REMINDERS

List additional tasks and reminders for the day.

☐ ....

☐ ....

☐ ....

☐ ....

☐ ....

☐ ....

6 ──────────────

7 ──────────────

8 ──────────────

9 ──────────────

10 ──────────────

11 ──────────────

12 ──────────────

1 ──────────────

2 ──────────────

3 ──────────────

4 ──────────────

5 ──────────────

6 ──────────────

7 ──────────────

In Progress   Completed

Deleted   Deferred

NOTES / IDEAS

Write down any notes or ideas you have today. For future reference, index them on page 5.

THURSDAY / /

MOST IMPORTANT TASK

What can you accomplish today to meet your
weekly objective?

☐ ....

SECONDARY TASK

These tasks can only be done after you've
completed your MIT

☐ ....

☐ ....

ADDITIONAL TASKS & REMINDERS

List additional tasks and reminders for the day.

☐ ....

☐ ....

☐ ....

☐ ....

☐ ....

☐ ....

▨ In Progress	▦ Completed
☒ Deleted	⇥ Deferred

6 ——————————————

7 ——————————————

8 ——————————————

9 ——————————————

10 ——————————————

11 ——————————————

12 ——————————————

1 ——————————————

2 ——————————————

3 ——————————————

4 ——————————————

5 ——————————————

6 ——————————————

7 ——————————————

NOTES / IDEAS

Write down any notes or ideas you have today. For future reference, index them on page 5.

FRIDAY / /

MOST IMPORTANT TASK

What can you accomplish today to meet your
weekly objective?

SECONDARY TASK

These tasks can only be done after you've
completed your MIT

ADDITIONAL TASKS & REMINDERS

List additional tasks and reminders for the day.

In Progress   Completed

Deleted   Deferred

6

7

8

9

10

11

12

1

2

3

4

5

6

7

NOTES / IDEAS

Write down any notes or ideas you have today. For future reference, index them on page 5.

SATURDAY / /

MOST IMPORTANT TASK

What can you accomplish today to meet your
weekly objective?

☐ ....

....

SECONDARY TASK

These tasks can only be done after you've
completed your MIT

☐ ....

☐ ....

ADDITIONAL TASKS & REMINDERS

List additional tasks and reminders for the day.

☐ ....

☐ ....

☐ ....

☐ ....

☐ ....

☐ ....

▨ In Progress	▨ Completed	
☒ Deleted	⇨ Deferred	

6 ————————————

7 --------------------

8 --------------------

9 --------------------

10 --------------------

11 --------------------

12 --------------------

1 --------------------

2 --------------------

3 --------------------

4 --------------------

5 --------------------

6 --------------------

7 --------------------

NOTES / IDEAS

Write down any notes or ideas you have today. For future reference, index them on page 5.

SUNDAY   /   /

MOST IMPORTANT TASK

What can you accomplish today to meet your
weekly objective?

☐ ....

....

SECONDARY TASK

These tasks can only be done after you've
completed your MIT

☐ ....

☐ ....

ADDITIONAL TASKS & REMINDERS

List additional tasks and reminders for the day.

☐ ....

☐ ....

☐ ....

☐ ....

☐ ....

☐ ....

▨ In Progress   ▦ Completed

☒ Deleted   ⇨ Deferred

6 —————————————————

7 ————————————————

8 ————————————————

9 ————————————————

10 ————————————————

11 ————————————————

12 ————————————————

1 ————————————————

2 ————————————————

3 ————————————————

4 ————————————————

5 ————————————————

6 ————————————————

7 ————————————————

NOTES / IDEAS

Write down any notes or ideas you have today. For future reference, index them on page 5.

WEEK 5 COMMITMENT

WEEKS LEFT IN QUARTER

`13` `12` `11` `10` `9` `8` `7` `6` `5` `4` `3` `2` `1`

Restate your goals each week to maintain your focus

PRIMARY GOAL

....

SECONDARY GOAL

....

TERTIARY GOAL

....

MUST-DELIVER TASK

What is the most relevant milestone in your Action Plan at the moment?
Towards achieving this milestone, what is the most important task you must finish this week?

☐ .... **A***

SECONDARY TASKS

List and prioritise secondary tasks using:

A = Must do this week
B = Good to do this week
C = Can do next week

☐ ....

☐ ....

☐ ....

☐ ....

☐ ....

☐ ....

Keep track of the progress you make on every task using these symbols:

⬚ In Progress   ⬛ Completed   ⊠ Deleted   ⇥ Deferred

AFTER-ACTION REVIEW

Review your results after completing your work week by answering the following questions:

HOW FAR DID YOU GET?
Evaluate your progress and visualise it using the progress bars.

PRIMARY GOAL	20%	40%	60%	80%
SECONDARY GOAL	20%	40%	60%	80%
TERTIARY GOAL	20%	40%	60%	80%

[ ] In Progress   [ ] Completed

WHAT IS WORKING?
List the activities you've completed in the past few weeks that you should focus on more.

1. ....

2. ....

3. ....

WHAT DIDN'T WORK?
List the activities that need to be fixed, improved, or removed.

1. ....

2. ....

3. ....

WHAT DID YOU LEARN?
Take a minute to reflect on the biggest takeaway from this week.

....

WEEK 5

MONDAY	TUESDAY	WEDNESDAY
7		
8		
9		
10		
11		
12		
1		
2		
3		
4		
5		
6		
7		

THURSDAY	FRIDAY	SAT	SUN
7			
8			
9			
10			
11			
12			
1			
2			
3			
4			
5			
6			
7			

MONDAY   /   /

MOST IMPORTANT TASK

What can you accomplish today to meet your
weekly objective?

☐ ....

....

SECONDARY TASK

These tasks can only be done after you've
completed your MIT

☐ ....

☐ ....

ADDITIONAL TASKS & REMINDERS

List additional tasks and reminders for the day.

☐ ....

☐ ....

☐ ....

☐ ....

☐ ....

☐ ....

▨ In Progress	▩ Completed
⊠ Deleted	⇨ Deferred

6 ─────────────────────

7 ─────────────────────

8 ─────────────────────

9 ─────────────────────

10 ─────────────────────

11 ─────────────────────

12 ─────────────────────

1 ─────────────────────

2 ─────────────────────

3 ─────────────────────

4 ─────────────────────

5 ─────────────────────

6 ─────────────────────

7 ─────────────────────

NOTES / IDEAS

Write down any notes or ideas you have today. For future reference, index them on page 5.

TUESDAY / /

MOST IMPORTANT TASK

What can you accomplish today to meet your
weekly objective?

☐ ....

SECONDARY TASK

These tasks can only be done after you've
completed your MIT

☐ ....

☐ ....

ADDITIONAL TASKS & REMINDERS

List additional tasks and reminders for the day.

☐ ....

☐ ....

☐ ....

☐ ....

☐ ....

☐ ....

▨ In Progress	▨ Completed		
☒ Deleted	⇨ Deferred		

6 ————————————

7 ————————————

8 ————————————

9 ————————————

10 ————————————

11 ————————————

12 ————————————

1 ————————————

2 ————————————

3 ————————————

4 ————————————

5 ————————————

6 ————————————

7 ————————————

NOTES / IDEAS

Write down any notes or ideas you have today. For future reference, index them on page 5.

....

....

....

....

....

....

....

....

....

....

....

....

....

....

....

....

....

....

....

....

....

....

....

....

....

....

....

....

....

....

WEDNESDAY   /   /

MOST IMPORTANT TASK

What can you accomplish today to meet your
weekly objective?

- [ ] ....

....

SECONDARY TASK

These tasks can only be done after you've
completed your MIT

- [ ] ....

- [ ] ....

ADDITIONAL TASKS & REMINDERS

List additional tasks and reminders for the day.

- [ ] ....

- [ ] ....

- [ ] ....

- [ ] ....

- [ ] ....

- [ ] ....

In Progress   Completed

Deleted   Deferred

6 ——————————————

7 ------------------------

8 ------------------------

9 ------------------------

10 ------------------------

11 ------------------------

12 ------------------------

1 ------------------------

2 ------------------------

3 ------------------------

4 ------------------------

5 ------------------------

6 ------------------------

7 ------------------------

NOTES / IDEAS

Write down any notes or ideas you have today. For future reference, index them on page 5.

THURSDAY / /

MOST IMPORTANT TASK
What can you accomplish today to meet your
weekly objective?

☐ ....

....

SECONDARY TASK
These tasks can only be done after you've
completed your MIT

☐ ....

☐ ....

ADDITIONAL TASKS & REMINDERS
List additional tasks and reminders for the day.

☐ ....

☐ ....

☐ ....

☐ ....

☐ ....

☐ ....

▨	In Progress	▦	Completed
⊠	Deleted	⇨	Deferred

6 ———————————————

7 - - - - - - - - - - - - - - - - -

8 - - - - - - - - - - - - - - - - -

9 - - - - - - - - - - - - - - - - -

10 - - - - - - - - - - - - - - - - -

11 - - - - - - - - - - - - - - - - -

12 - - - - - - - - - - - - - - - - -

1 - - - - - - - - - - - - - - - - -

2 - - - - - - - - - - - - - - - - -

3 - - - - - - - - - - - - - - - - -

4 - - - - - - - - - - - - - - - - -

5 - - - - - - - - - - - - - - - - -

6 - - - - - - - - - - - - - - - - -

7 - - - - - - - - - - - - - - - - -

NOTES / IDEAS

Write down any notes or ideas you have today. For future reference, index them on page 5.

FRIDAY   /   /

MOST IMPORTANT TASK

What can you accomplish today to meet your
weekly objective?

☐ ....

....

SECONDARY TASK

These tasks can only be done after you've
completed your MIT

☐ ....

☐ ....

ADDITIONAL TASKS & REMINDERS

List additional tasks and reminders for the day.

☐ ....

☐ ....

☐ ....

☐ ....

☐ ....

☐ ....

🔲 In Progress   ⬛ Completed

☒ Deleted   ⇥ Deferred

6 ———————————————

7 -------------------------

8 -------------------------

9 -------------------------

10 -------------------------

11 -------------------------

12 -------------------------

1 -------------------------

2 -------------------------

3 -------------------------

4 -------------------------

5 -------------------------

6 -------------------------

7 -------------------------

NOTES / IDEAS

Write down any notes or ideas you have today. For future reference, index them on page 5.

SATURDAY   /   /

MOST IMPORTANT TASK
What can you accomplish today to meet your
weekly objective?

☐ ....

SECONDARY TASK
These tasks can only be done after you've
completed your MIT

☐ ....

☐ ....

ADDITIONAL TASKS & REMINDERS
List additional tasks and reminders for the day.

☐ ....

☐ ....

☐ ....

☐ ....

☐ ....

☐ ....

In Progress   Completed

Deleted   Deferred

6 ——————————

7 ------------------------

8 ------------------------

9 ------------------------

10 ------------------------

11 ------------------------

12 ------------------------

1 ------------------------

2 ------------------------

3 ------------------------

4 ------------------------

5 ------------------------

6 ------------------------

7 ------------------------

NOTES / IDEAS

Write down any notes or ideas you have today. For future reference, index them on page 5.

SUNDAY   /   /

Schedule blocks of time to complete
your tasks and reminders

MOST IMPORTANT TASK
What can you accomplish today to meet your
weekly objective?

☐ ....

....

SECONDARY TASK
These tasks can only be done after you've
completed your MIT

☐ ....

☐ ....

ADDITIONAL TASKS & REMINDERS
List additional tasks and reminders for the day.

☐ ....

☐ ....

☐ ....

☐ ....

☐ ....

☐ ....

In Progress   Completed

Deleted   Deferred

6 ————————

7 ---------------

8 ---------------

9 ---------------

10 --------------

11 --------------

12 --------------

1 ---------------

2 ---------------

3 ---------------

4 ---------------

5 ---------------

6 ---------------

7 ---------------

NOTES / IDEAS

Write down any notes or ideas you have today. For future reference, index them on page 5.

WEEK 6 COMMITMENT

WEEKS LEFT IN QUARTER

13 12 11 10 9 8 7 6 5 4 3 2 1

Restate your goals each week to maintain your focus

PRIMARY GOAL

....

SECONDARY GOAL

....

TERTIARY GOAL

....

MUST-DELIVER TASK

What is the most relevant milestone in your Action Plan at the moment?
Towards achieving this milestone, what is the most important task you must finish this week?

☐ .... **A***

SECONDARY TASKS

List and prioritise secondary tasks using:

A = Must do this week

B = Good to do this week

C = Can do next week

☐ ....

☐ ....

☐ ....

☐ ....

☐ ....

☐ ....

Keep track of the progress you make on every task using these symbols:

⬚ In Progress ⬛ Completed ☒ Deleted ⇨ Deferred

AFTER-ACTION REVIEW

Review your results after completing your work week by answering the following questions:

HOW FAR DID YOU GET?
Evaluate your progress and visualise it using the progress bars.

PRIMARY GOAL	20%	40%	60%	80%	
SECONDARY GOAL	20%	40%	60%	80%	
TERTIARY GOAL	20%	40%	60%	80%	

[ ] In Progress   [ ] Completed

WHAT IS WORKING?
List the activities you've completed in the past few weeks that you should focus on more.

1. ....

2. ....

3. ....

WHAT DIDN'T WORK?
List the activities that need to be fixed, improved, or removed.

1. ....

2. ....

3. ....

WHAT DID YOU LEARN?
Take a minute to reflect on the biggest takeaway from this week.

....

WEEK 6

MONDAY	TUESDAY	WEDNESDAY
7		
8		
9		
10		
11		
12		
1		
2		
3		
4		
5		
6		
7		

THURSDAY	FRIDAY	SAT	SUN
7			
8			
9			
10			
11			
12			
1			
2			
3			
4			
5			
6			
7			

MONDAY   /   /

MOST IMPORTANT TASK

What can you accomplish today to meet your
weekly objective?

☐ ....

SECONDARY TASK

These tasks can only be done after you've
completed your MIT

☐ ....

☐ ....

ADDITIONAL TASKS & REMINDERS

List additional tasks and reminders for the day.

☐ ....

☐ ....

☐ ....

☐ ....

☐ ....

☐ ....

In Progress   Completed

Deleted   Deferred

6 ————————————

7 ---------------------------

8 ---------------------------

9 ---------------------------

10 --------------------------

11 --------------------------

12 --------------------------

1 ---------------------------

2 ---------------------------

3 ---------------------------

4 ---------------------------

5 ---------------------------

6 ---------------------------

7 ---------------------------

NOTES / IDEAS

Write down any notes or ideas you have today. For future reference, index them on page 5.

TUESDAY   /   /

MOST IMPORTANT TASK

What can you accomplish today to meet your
weekly objective?

☐ ....

....

SECONDARY TASK

These tasks can only be done after you've
completed your MIT

☐ ....

☐ ....

ADDITIONAL TASKS & REMINDERS

List additional tasks and reminders for the day.

☐ ....

☐ ....

☐ ....

☐ ....

☐ ....

☐ ....

◪ In Progress   ▨ Completed

☒ Deleted   ⇨ Deferred

6 ————————————————

7 ————————————————

8 ————————————————

9 ————————————————

10 ————————————————

11 ————————————————

12 ————————————————

1 ————————————————

2 ————————————————

3 ————————————————

4 ————————————————

5 ————————————————

6 ————————————————

7 ————————————————

NOTES / IDEAS

Write down any notes or ideas you have today. For future reference, index them on page 5.

WEDNESDAY / /

MOST IMPORTANT TASK
What can you accomplish today to meet your weekly objective?

☐ ....

SECONDARY TASK
These tasks can only be done after you've completed your MIT

☐ ....

☐ ....

ADDITIONAL TASKS & REMINDERS
List additional tasks and reminders for the day.

☐ ....

☐ ....

☐ ....

☐ ....

☐ ....

☐ ....

| ▧ In Progress | ▩ Completed |
| ⊠ Deleted | ⇨ Deferred |

6 ——————————————

7 ------------------------------

8 ------------------------------

9 ------------------------------

10 ------------------------------

11 ------------------------------

12 ------------------------------

1 ------------------------------

2 ------------------------------

3 ------------------------------

4 ------------------------------

5 ------------------------------

6 ------------------------------

7 ------------------------------

NOTES / IDEAS

Write down any notes or ideas you have today. For future reference, index them on page 5.

THURSDAY / /

MOST IMPORTANT TASK
What can you accomplish today to meet your
weekly objective?

☐ ....

....

SECONDARY TASK
These tasks can only be done after you've
completed your MIT

☐ ....

☐ ....

ADDITIONAL TASKS & REMINDERS
List additional tasks and reminders for the day.

☐ ....

☐ ....

☐ ....

☐ ....

☐ ....

☐ ....

☑ In Progress   ▨ Completed

☒ Deleted   ⇨ Deferred

6 ─────────────────

7 ─────────────────

8 ─────────────────

9 ─────────────────

10 ─────────────────

11 ─────────────────

12 ─────────────────

1 ─────────────────

2 ─────────────────

3 ─────────────────

4 ─────────────────

5 ─────────────────

6 ─────────────────

7 ─────────────────

NOTES / IDEAS

Write down any notes or ideas you have today. For future reference, index them on page 5.

FRIDAY / /

MOST IMPORTANT TASK
What can you accomplish today to meet your
weekly objective?

- [ ]

SECONDARY TASK
These tasks can only be done after you've
completed your MIT

- [ ]
- [ ]

ADDITIONAL TASKS & REMINDERS
List additional tasks and reminders for the day.

- [ ]
- [ ]
- [ ]
- [ ]
- [ ]
- [ ]

In Progress   Completed
Deleted   Deferred

6

7

8

9

10

11

12

1

2

3

4

5

6

7

NOTES / IDEAS

Write down any notes or ideas you have today. For future reference, index them on page 5.

....

....

....

....

....

....

....

....

....

....

....

....

....

....

....

....

....

....

....

....

....

....

....

....

....

....

....

....

....

....

SATURDAY / /

Schedule blocks of time to complete
your tasks and reminders

MOST IMPORTANT TASK
What can you accomplish today to meet your
weekly objective?

☐ ....

....

SECONDARY TASK
These tasks can only be done after you've
completed your MIT

☐ ....

☐ ....

ADDITIONAL TASKS & REMINDERS
List additional tasks and reminders for the day.

☐ ....

☐ ....

☐ ....

☐ ....

☐ ....

☐ ....

▨ In Progress   ▨ Completed

☒ Deleted   ☐⇥ Deferred

6 ————————————————

7 ----------------------

8 ----------------------

9 ----------------------

10 ----------------------

11 ----------------------

12 ----------------------

1 ----------------------

2 ----------------------

3 ----------------------

4 ----------------------

5 ----------------------

6 ----------------------

7 ----------------------

NOTES / IDEAS

Write down any notes or ideas you have today. For future reference, index them on page 5.

SUNDAY   /   /

MOST IMPORTANT TASK

What can you accomplish today to meet your
weekly objective?

☐ ....

SECONDARY TASK

These tasks can only be done after you've
completed your MIT

☐ ....

☐ ....

ADDITIONAL TASKS & REMINDERS

List additional tasks and reminders for the day.

☐ ....

☐ ....

☐ ....

☐ ....

☐ ....

☐ ....

	In Progress		Completed
	Deleted		Deferred

6 ————————————

7 ————————————

8 ————————————

9 ————————————

10 ————————————

11 ————————————

12 ————————————

1 ————————————

2 ————————————

3 ————————————

4 ————————————

5 ————————————

6 ————————————

7 ————————————

NOTES / IDEAS

Write down any notes or ideas you have today. For future reference, index them on page 5.

WEEK 7 COMMITMENT

WEEKS LEFT IN QUARTER

`13` `12` `11` `10` `9` `8` `7` `6` `5` `4` `3` `2` `1`

Restate your goals each week to maintain your focus

PRIMARY GOAL

....

SECONDARY GOAL

....

TERTIARY GOAL

....

MUST-DELIVER TASK

What is the most relevant milestone in your Action Plan at the moment?
Towards achieving this milestone, what is the most important task you must finish this week?

☐ .... **A***

SECONDARY TASKS

List and prioritise secondary tasks using:

A = Must do this week

B = Good to do this week

C = Can do next week

☐ ....

☐ ....

☐ ....

☐ ....

☐ ....

☐ ....

Keep track of the progress you make on every task using these symbols:

☐ In Progress   ☐ Completed   ☒ Deleted   ☐⇒ Deferred

AFTER-ACTION REVIEW

Review your results after completing your work week by answering the following questions:

HOW FAR DID YOU GET?

Evaluate your progress and visualise it using the progress bars.

PRIMARY GOAL	20%	40%	60%	80%
SECONDARY GOAL	20%	40%	60%	80%
TERTIARY GOAL	20%	40%	60%	80%

☐ In Progress   ☐ Completed

WHAT IS WORKING?

List the activities you've completed in the past few weeks that you should focus on more.

1. _____

2. _____

3. _____

WHAT DIDN'T WORK?

List the activities that need to be fixed, improved, or removed.

1. _____

2. _____

3. _____

WHAT DID YOU LEARN?

Take a minute to reflect on the biggest takeaway from this week.

_____

WEEK 7

MONDAY	TUESDAY	WEDNESDAY
7		
8		
9		
10		
11		
12		
1		
2		
3		
4		
5		
6		
7		

THURSDAY	FRIDAY	SAT	SUN
7			
8			
9			
10			
11			
12			
1			
2			
3			
4			
5			
6			
7			

MONDAY   /   /

MOST IMPORTANT TASK

What can you accomplish today to meet your
weekly objective?

☐ ....

....

SECONDARY TASK

These tasks can only be done after you've
completed your MIT

☐ ....

☐ ....

ADDITIONAL TASKS & REMINDERS

List additional tasks and reminders for the day.

☐ ....

☐ ....

☐ ....

☐ ....

☐ ....

☐ ....

▨ In Progress	▨ Completed
☒ Deleted	⇨ Deferred

6 ───────────────

7 ───────────────

8 ───────────────

9 ───────────────

10 ───────────────

11 ───────────────

12 ───────────────

1 ───────────────

2 ───────────────

3 ───────────────

4 ───────────────

5 ───────────────

6 ───────────────

7 ───────────────

NOTES / IDEAS

Write down any notes or ideas you have today. For future reference, index them on page 5.

TUESDAY / /

MOST IMPORTANT TASK

What can you accomplish today to meet your
weekly objective?

☐ ....

SECONDARY TASK

These tasks can only be done after you've
completed your MIT

☐ ....

☐ ....

ADDITIONAL TASKS & REMINDERS

List additional tasks and reminders for the day.

☐ ....

☐ ....

☐ ....

☐ ....

☐ ....

☐ ....

▣ In Progress	▣ Completed
☒ Deleted	⇨ Deferred

6 ————————————

7 ------------------------

8 ------------------------

9 ------------------------

10 ------------------------

11 ------------------------

12 ------------------------

1 ------------------------

2 ------------------------

3 ------------------------

4 ------------------------

5 ------------------------

6 ------------------------

7 ------------------------

NOTES / IDEAS

Write down any notes or ideas you have today. For future reference, index them on page 5.

WEDNESDAY / /

MOST IMPORTANT TASK
What can you accomplish today to meet your
weekly objective?

☐ ....

SECONDARY TASK
These tasks can only be done after you've
completed your MIT

☐ ....

☐ ....

ADDITIONAL TASKS & REMINDERS
List additional tasks and reminders for the day.

☐ ....

☐ ....

☐ ....

☐ ....

☐ ....

☐ ....

▨ In Progress	▨ Completed
⊠ Deleted	⇨ Deferred

6 ——————————————

7 ——————————————

8 ——————————————

9 ——————————————

10 ——————————————

11 ——————————————

12 ——————————————

1 ——————————————

2 ——————————————

3 ——————————————

4 ——————————————

5 ——————————————

6 ——————————————

7 ——————————————

NOTES / IDEAS

Write down any notes or ideas you have today. For future reference, index them on page 5.

THURSDAY / /

MOST IMPORTANT TASK

What can you accomplish today to meet your
weekly objective?

☐ ....

SECONDARY TASK

These tasks can only be done after you've
completed your MIT

☐ ....

☐ ....

ADDITIONAL TASKS & REMINDERS

List additional tasks and reminders for the day.

☐ ....

☐ ....

☐ ....

☐ ....

☐ ....

☐ ....

▨ In Progress   ▧ Completed

☒ Deleted   ⇨ Deferred

6 ——————————————

7 ——————————————

8 ——————————————

9 ——————————————

10 ——————————————

11 ——————————————

12 ——————————————

1 ——————————————

2 ——————————————

3 ——————————————

4 ——————————————

5 ——————————————

6 ——————————————

7 ——————————————

NOTES / IDEAS

Write down any notes or ideas you have today. For future reference, index them on page 5.

FRIDAY   /   /

MOST IMPORTANT TASK

What can you accomplish today to meet your
weekly objective?

☐ ....

SECONDARY TASK

These tasks can only be done after you've
completed your MIT

☐ ....

☐ ....

ADDITIONAL TASKS & REMINDERS

List additional tasks and reminders for the day.

☐ ....

☐ ....

☐ ....

☐ ....

☐ ....

☐ ....

| ◨ In Progress | ▨ Completed |
| ⊠ Deleted | ⇨ Deferred |

6

7

8

9

10

11

12

1

2

3

4

5

6

7

NOTES / IDEAS

Write down any notes or ideas you have today. For future reference, index them on page 5.

SATURDAY / /

MOST IMPORTANT TASK

What can you accomplish today to meet your
weekly objective?

☐ ....

SECONDARY TASK

These tasks can only be done after you've
completed your MIT

☐ ....

☐ ....

ADDITIONAL TASKS & REMINDERS

List additional tasks and reminders for the day.

☐ ....

☐ ....

☐ ....

☐ ....

☐ ....

☐ ....

	In Progress		Completed
☒	Deleted	⇨	Deferred

6 ————————

7 ————————

8 ————————

9 ————————

10 ————————

11 ————————

12 ————————

1 ————————

2 ————————

3 ————————

4 ————————

5 ————————

6 ————————

7 ————————

NOTES / IDEAS

Write down any notes or ideas you have today. For future reference, index them on page 5.

SUNDAY   /   /

MOST IMPORTANT TASK
What can you accomplish today to meet your weekly objective?

☐ ....

....

SECONDARY TASK
These tasks can only be done after you've completed your MIT

☐ ....

☐ ....

ADDITIONAL TASKS & REMINDERS
List additional tasks and reminders for the day.

☐ ....

☐ ....

☐ ....

☐ ....

☐ ....

☐ ....

▨ In Progress   ▨ Completed

☒ Deleted   ⇨ Deferred

6 ——————————————

7 ————————————————

8 ————————————————

9 ————————————————

10 ———————————————

11 ———————————————

12 ———————————————

1 ————————————————

2 ————————————————

3 ————————————————

4 ————————————————

5 ————————————————

6 ————————————————

7 ————————————————

NOTES / IDEAS

Write down any notes or ideas you have today. For future reference, index them on page 5.

WEEK 8 COMMITMENT

WEEKS LEFT IN QUARTER

`13` `12` `11` `10` `9` `8` `7` `6` `5` `4` `3` `2` `1`

Restate your goals each week to maintain your focus

PRIMARY GOAL

....

SECONDARY GOAL

....

TERTIARY GOAL

....

MUST-DELIVER TASK

What is the most relevant milestone in your Action Plan at the moment?
Towards achieving this milestone, what is the most important task you must finish this week?

☐ .... **A***

SECONDARY TASKS

List and prioritise secondary tasks using:

A = Must do this week

B = Good to do this week

C = Can do next week

☐ ....

☐ ....

☐ ....

☐ ....

☐ ....

☐ ....

Keep track of the progress you make on every task using these symbols:

☑ In Progress   ☑ Completed   ☒ Deleted   ⟶ Deferred

AFTER-ACTION REVIEW

Review your results after completing your work week by answering the following questions:

HOW FAR DID YOU GET?
Evaluate your progress and visualise it using the progress bars.

PRIMARY GOAL	20%	40%	60%	80%
SECONDARY GOAL	20%	40%	60%	80%
TERTIARY GOAL	20%	40%	60%	80%

☐ In Progress   ☐ Completed

WHAT IS WORKING?
List the activities you've completed in the past few weeks that you should focus on more.

1. _____

2. _____

3. _____

WHAT DIDN'T WORK?
List the activities that need to be fixed, improved, or removed.

1. _____

2. _____

3. _____

WHAT DID YOU LEARN?
Take a minute to reflect on the biggest takeaway from this week.

_____

WEEK 8

	MONDAY	TUESDAY	WEDNESDAY
7			
8			
9			
10			
11			
12			
1			
2			
3			
4			
5			
6			
7			

THURSDAY	FRIDAY	SAT	SUN
7			
8			
9			
10			
11			
12			
1			
2			
3			
4			
5			
6			
7			

MONDAY / /

MOST IMPORTANT TASK

What can you accomplish today to meet your
weekly objective?

SECONDARY TASK

These tasks can only be done after you've
completed your MIT

ADDITIONAL TASKS & REMINDERS

List additional tasks and reminders for the day.

In Progress   Completed

Deleted   Deferred

6

7

8

9

10

11

12

1

2

3

4

5

6

7

NOTES / IDEAS

Write down any notes or ideas you have today. For future reference, index them on page 5.

TUESDAY / /

Schedule blocks of time to complete
your tasks and reminders

MOST IMPORTANT TASK

What can you accomplish today to meet your
weekly objective?

☐ ....

SECONDARY TASK

These tasks can only be done after you've
completed your MIT

☐ ....

☐ ....

ADDITIONAL TASKS & REMINDERS

List additional tasks and reminders for the day.

☐ ....

☐ ....

☐ ....

☐ ....

☐ ....

☐ ....

☑ In Progress   ▩ Completed

☒ Deleted   ⇨ Deferred

6 ——————————————

7 ——————————————

8 ——————————————

9 ——————————————

10 ——————————————

11 ——————————————

12 ——————————————

1 ——————————————

2 ——————————————

3 ——————————————

4 ——————————————

5 ——————————————

6 ——————————————

7 ——————————————

NOTES / IDEAS

Write down any notes or ideas you have today. For future reference, index them on page 5.

WEDNESDAY   /   /

MOST IMPORTANT TASK

What can you accomplish today to meet your weekly objective?

☐ ....

SECONDARY TASK

These tasks can only be done after you've completed your MIT

☐ ....

☐ ....

ADDITIONAL TASKS & REMINDERS

List additional tasks and reminders for the day.

☐ ....

☐ ....

☐ ....

☐ ....

☐ ....

☐ ....

In Progress Completed

Deleted Deferred

6 ——————————

7 ——————————

8 ——————————

9 ——————————

10 ——————————

11 ——————————

12 ——————————

1 ——————————

2 ——————————

3 ——————————

4 ——————————

5 ——————————

6 ——————————

7 ——————————

NOTES / IDEAS

Write down any notes or ideas you have today. For future reference, index them on page 5.

THURSDAY   /   /

MOST IMPORTANT TASK

What can you accomplish today to meet your
weekly objective?

SECONDARY TASK

These tasks can only be done after you've
completed your MIT

ADDITIONAL TASKS & REMINDERS

List additional tasks and reminders for the day.

6
7
8
9
10
11
12
1
2
3
4
5
6
7

In Progress   Completed

Deleted   Deferred

NOTES / IDEAS

Write down any notes or ideas you have today. For future reference, index them on page 5.

FRIDAY   /   /

Schedule blocks of time to complete
your tasks and reminders

MOST IMPORTANT TASK

What can you accomplish today to meet your
weekly objective?

☐ ....

....

SECONDARY TASK

These tasks can only be done after you've
completed your MIT

☐ ....

☐ ....

ADDITIONAL TASKS & REMINDERS

List additional tasks and reminders for the day.

☐ ....

☐ ....

☐ ....

☐ ....

☐ ....

☐ ....

☑ In Progress   ▦ Completed

☒ Deleted   ⇨ Deferred

6 ————————————————

7 ————————————————

8 ————————————————

9 ————————————————

10 ————————————————

11 ————————————————

12 ————————————————

1 ————————————————

2 ————————————————

3 ————————————————

4 ————————————————

5 ————————————————

6 ————————————————

7 ————————————————

NOTES / IDEAS

Write down any notes or ideas you have today. For future reference, index them on page 5.

SATURDAY / /

MOST IMPORTANT TASK
What can you accomplish today to meet your
weekly objective?

☐ ....

SECONDARY TASK
These tasks can only be done after you've
completed your MIT

☐ ....

☐ ....

ADDITIONAL TASKS & REMINDERS
List additional tasks and reminders for the day.

☐ ....

☐ ....

☐ ....

☐ ....

☐ ....

☐ ....

☑ In Progress   ☒ Completed

☒ Deleted   ☒ Deferred

6 ————————————

7 ————————————

8 ————————————

9 ————————————

10 ————————————

11 ————————————

12 ————————————

1 ————————————

2 ————————————

3 ————————————

4 ————————————

5 ————————————

6 ————————————

7 ————————————

NOTES / IDEAS

Write down any notes or ideas you have today. For future reference, index them on page 5.

....

....

....

....

....

....

....

....

....

....

....

....

....

....

....

....

....

....

....

....

....

....

....

....

....

....

....

....

....

....

SUNDAY   /   /

Schedule blocks of time to complete
your tasks and reminders

MOST IMPORTANT TASK

What can you accomplish today to meet your
weekly objective?

☐ ....

SECONDARY TASK

These tasks can only be done after you've
completed your MIT

☐ ....

☐ ....

ADDITIONAL TASKS & REMINDERS

List additional tasks and reminders for the day.

☐ ....

☐ ....

☐ ....

☐ ....

☐ ....

☐ ....

▨ In Progress   ▨ Completed
⊠ Deleted   ⇨ Deferred

6 ————————————

7 ————————————

8 ————————————

9 ————————————

10 ————————————

11 ————————————

12 ————————————

1 ————————————

2 ————————————

3 ————————————

4 ————————————

5 ————————————

6 ————————————

7 ————————————

NOTES / IDEAS

Write down any notes or ideas you have today. For future reference, index them on page 5.

WEEK 9 COMMITMENT

`13` `12` `11` `10` `9` `8` `7` `6` `5` **4** **3** **2** **1**

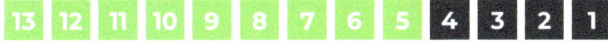

Restate your goals each week to maintain your focus

PRIMARY GOAL

....

SECONDARY GOAL

....

TERTIARY GOAL

....

MUST-DELIVER TASK

What is the most relevant milestone in your Action Plan at the moment?
Towards achieving this milestone, what is the most important task you must finish this week?

☐ .... **A***

SECONDARY TASKS

List and prioritise secondary tasks using:

A = Must do this week

B = Good to do this week

C = Can do next week

☐ ....

☐ ....

☐ ....

☐ ....

☐ ....

☐ ....

Keep track of the progress you make on every task using these symbols:

▨ In Progress   ▨ Completed   ⊠ Deleted   ⇨ Deferred

AFTER-ACTION REVIEW

Review your results after completing your work week by answering the following questions:

HOW FAR DID YOU GET?

Evaluate your progress and visualise it using the progress bars.

PRIMARY GOAL	20%	40%	60%	80%
SECONDARY GOAL	20%	40%	60%	80%
TERTIARY GOAL	20%	40%	60%	80%

☐ In Progress   ☐ Completed

WHAT IS WORKING?

List the activities you've completed in the past few weeks that you should focus on more.

1. ....

2. ....

3. ....

WHAT DIDN'T WORK?

List the activities that need to be fixed, improved, or removed.

1. ....

2. ....

3. ....

WHAT DID YOU LEARN?

Take a minute to reflect on the biggest takeaway from this week.

....

WEEK 9

MONDAY	TUESDAY	WEDNESDAY
7		
8		
9		
10		
11		
12		
1		
2		
3		
4		
5		
6		
7		

THURSDAY	FRIDAY	SAT	SUN
7			
8			
9			
10			
11			
12			
1			
2			
3			
4			
5			
6			
7			

MONDAY   /   /

MOST IMPORTANT TASK

What can you accomplish today to meet your weekly objective?

☐ ....

SECONDARY TASK

These tasks can only be done after you've completed your MIT

☐ ....

☐ ....

ADDITIONAL TASKS & REMINDERS

List additional tasks and reminders for the day.

☐ ....

☐ ....

☐ ....

☐ ....

☐ ....

☐ ....

▨ In Progress   ▦ Completed

☒ Deleted   ⇨ Deferred

6 ———————————————

7 ————————————————

8 ————————————————

9 ————————————————

10 ———————————————

11 ————————————————

12 ————————————————

1 ————————————————

2 ————————————————

3 ————————————————

4 ————————————————

5 ————————————————

6 ————————————————

7 ————————————————

NOTES / IDEAS

Write down any notes or ideas you have today. For future reference, index them on page 5.

TUESDAY / /

Schedule blocks of time to complete
your tasks and reminders

MOST IMPORTANT TASK

What can you accomplish today to meet your
weekly objective?

☐ ....

....

SECONDARY TASK

These tasks can only be done after you've
completed your MIT

☐ ....

☐ ....

ADDITIONAL TASKS & REMINDERS

List additional tasks and reminders for the day.

☐ ....

☐ ....

☐ ....

☐ ....

☐ ....

☐ ....

▨ In Progress ▨ Completed

☒ Deleted ⇨ Deferred

6 ————————————

7 ————————————

8 ————————————

9 ————————————

10 ————————————

11 ————————————

12 ————————————

1 ————————————

2 ————————————

3 ————————————

4 ————————————

5 ————————————

6 ————————————

7 ————————————

NOTES / IDEAS

Write down any notes or ideas you have today. For future reference, index them on page 5.

WEDNESDAY / /

MOST IMPORTANT TASK

What can you accomplish today to meet your
weekly objective?

☐ ....

....

SECONDARY TASK

These tasks can only be done after you've
completed your MIT

☐ ....

☐ ....

ADDITIONAL TASKS & REMINDERS

List additional tasks and reminders for the day.

☐ ....

☐ ....

☐ ....

☐ ....

☐ ....

☐ ....

▨ In Progress   ▨ Completed

☒ Deleted   ⇨ Deferred

6 ————————————————

7 ————————————————

8 ————————————————

9 ————————————————

10 ————————————————

11 ————————————————

12 ————————————————

1 ————————————————

2 ————————————————

3 ————————————————

4 ————————————————

5 ————————————————

6 ————————————————

7 ————————————————

NOTES / IDEAS

Write down any notes or ideas you have today. For future reference, index them on page 5.

THURSDAY / /

MOST IMPORTANT TASK

What can you accomplish today to meet your
weekly objective?

☐ ....

SECONDARY TASK

These tasks can only be done after you've
completed your MIT

☐ ....

☐ ....

ADDITIONAL TASKS & REMINDERS

List additional tasks and reminders for the day.

☐ ....

☐ ....

☐ ....

☐ ....

☐ ....

☐ ....

☑ In Progress   ▦ Completed

☒ Deleted   ☐⇨ Deferred

6 ————————————————

7 ————————————————

8 ————————————————

9 ————————————————

10 ————————————————

11 ————————————————

12 ————————————————

1 ————————————————

2 ————————————————

3 ————————————————

4 ————————————————

5 ————————————————

6 ————————————————

7 ————————————————

NOTES / IDEAS

Write down any notes or ideas you have today. For future reference, index them on page 5.

FRIDAY   /   /

MOST IMPORTANT TASK

What can you accomplish today to meet your
weekly objective?

☐ ....

....

SECONDARY TASK

These tasks can only be done after you've
completed your MIT

☐ ....

☐ ....

ADDITIONAL TASKS & REMINDERS

List additional tasks and reminders for the day.

☐ ....

☐ ....

☐ ....

☐ ....

☐ ....

☐ ....

▨ In Progress   ▨ Completed

☒ Deleted   ⇨ Deferred

6 ——————————

7 ------------------

8 ------------------

9 ------------------

10 ------------------

11 ------------------

12 ------------------

1 ------------------

2 ------------------

3 ------------------

4 ------------------

5 ------------------

6 ------------------

7 ------------------

NOTES / IDEAS

Write down any notes or ideas you have today. For future reference, index them on page 5.

SATURDAY / /

MOST IMPORTANT TASK

What can you accomplish today to meet your
weekly objective?

☐ ....

SECONDARY TASK

These tasks can only be done after you've
completed your MIT

☐ ....

☐ ....

ADDITIONAL TASKS & REMINDERS

List additional tasks and reminders for the day.

☐ ....

☐ ....

☐ ....

☐ ....

☐ ....

☐ ....

☑ In Progress   ▨ Completed

☒ Deleted   ⇨ Deferred

6 ——————————————

7 ——————————————

8 ——————————————

9 ——————————————

10 ——————————————

11 ——————————————

12 ——————————————

1 ——————————————

2 ——————————————

3 ——————————————

4 ——————————————

5 ——————————————

6 ——————————————

7 ——————————————

NOTES / IDEAS

Write down any notes or ideas you have today. For future reference, index them on page 5.

SUNDAY / /

MOST IMPORTANT TASK

What can you accomplish today to meet your weekly objective?

☐ ....

SECONDARY TASK

These tasks can only be done after you've completed your MIT

☐ ....

☐ ....

ADDITIONAL TASKS & REMINDERS

List additional tasks and reminders for the day.

☐ ....

☐ ....

☐ ....

☐ ....

☐ ....

☐ ....

▨ In Progress   ▩ Completed

☒ Deleted   ⇨ Deferred

6 —————————————

7 ————————————

8 ————————————

9 ————————————

10 ————————————

11 ————————————

12 ————————————

1 ————————————

2 ————————————

3 ————————————

4 ————————————

5 ————————————

6 ————————————

7 ————————————

NOTES / IDEAS

Write down any notes or ideas you have today. For future reference, index them on page 5.

WEEK 10 COMMITMENT

WEEKS LEFT IN QUARTER

`13` `12` `11` `10` `9` `8` `7` `6` `5` `4` `3` `2` `1`

Restate your goals each week to maintain your focus

PRIMARY GOAL

....

SECONDARY GOAL

....

TERTIARY GOAL

....

MUST-DELIVER TASK

What is the most relevant milestone in your Action Plan at the moment?
Towards achieving this milestone, what is the most important task you must finish this week?

☐ .... **A***

SECONDARY TASKS

List and prioritise secondary tasks using:

A = Must do this week

B = Good to do this week

C = Can do next week

☐ .... |

☐ .... |

☐ .... |

☐ .... |

☐ .... |

☐ .... |

Keep track of the progress you make on every task using these symbols:

☑ In Progress   ☑ Completed   ☒ Deleted   ☐⇨ Deferred

AFTER-ACTION REVIEW

Review your results after completing your work week by answering the following questions:

HOW FAR DID YOU GET?
Evaluate your progress and visualise it using the progress bars.

PRIMARY GOAL	20%	40%	60%	80%
SECONDARY GOAL	20%	40%	60%	80%
TERTIARY GOAL	20%	40%	60%	80%

In Progress   Completed

WHAT IS WORKING?
List the activities you've completed in the past few weeks that you should focus on more.

1. ....

2. ....

3. ....

WHAT DIDN'T WORK?
List the activities that need to be fixed, improved, or removed.

1. ....

2. ....

3. ....

WHAT DID YOU LEARN?
Take a minute to reflect on the biggest takeaway from this week.

....

WEEK 10

MONDAY	TUESDAY	WEDNESDAY
7		
8		
9		
10		
11		
12		
1		
2		
3		
4		
5		
6		
7		

THURSDAY	FRIDAY	SAT	SUN
7			
8			
9			
10			
11			
12			
1			
2			
3			
4			
5			
6			
7			

MONDAY / /

MOST IMPORTANT TASK

What can you accomplish today to meet your
weekly objective?

☐ ....

SECONDARY TASK

These tasks can only be done after you've
completed your MIT

☐ ....

☐ ....

ADDITIONAL TASKS & REMINDERS

List additional tasks and reminders for the day.

☐ ....

☐ ....

☐ ....

☐ ....

☐ ....

☐ ....

▨ In Progress   ▩ Completed

▧ Deleted   ▭⇨ Deferred

6 —————————————————

7 —————————————————

8 —————————————————

9 —————————————————

10 —————————————————

11 —————————————————

12 —————————————————

1 —————————————————

2 —————————————————

3 —————————————————

4 —————————————————

5 —————————————————

6 —————————————————

7 —————————————————

NOTES / IDEAS

Write down any notes or ideas you have today. For future reference, index them on page 5.

TUESDAY / /

Schedule blocks of time to complete your tasks and reminders

MOST IMPORTANT TASK

What can you accomplish today to meet your weekly objective?

SECONDARY TASK

These tasks can only be done after you've completed your MIT

ADDITIONAL TASKS & REMINDERS

List additional tasks and reminders for the day.

In Progress

Completed

Deleted

Deferred

6

7

8

9

10

11

12

1

2

3

4

5

6

7

NOTES / IDEAS

Write down any notes or ideas you have today. For future reference, index them on page 5.

WEDNESDAY / /

MOST IMPORTANT TASK

What can you accomplish today to meet your
weekly objective?

SECONDARY TASK

These tasks can only be done after you've
completed your MIT

ADDITIONAL TASKS & REMINDERS

List additional tasks and reminders for the day.

In Progress   Completed

Deleted   Deferred

6

7

8

9

10

11

12

1

2

3

4

5

6

7

NOTES / IDEAS

Write down any notes or ideas you have today. For future reference, index them on page 5.

THURSDAY / /

MOST IMPORTANT TASK

What can you accomplish today to meet your
weekly objective?

☐ ....

....

SECONDARY TASK

These tasks can only be done after you've
completed your MIT

☐ ....

☐ ....

ADDITIONAL TASKS & REMINDERS

List additional tasks and reminders for the day.

☐ ....

☐ ....

☐ ....

☐ ....

☐ ....

☐ ....

⬚ In Progress	⬛ Completed
⊠ Deleted	⇨ Deferred

6 ————————————

7 ————————————

8 ————————————

9 ————————————

10 ————————————

11 ————————————

12 ————————————

1 ————————————

2 ————————————

3 ————————————

4 ————————————

5 ————————————

6 ————————————

7 ————————————

NOTES / IDEAS

Write down any notes or ideas you have today. For future reference, index them on page 5.

FRIDAY / /

MOST IMPORTANT TASK

What can you accomplish today to meet your
weekly objective?

☐ ....

SECONDARY TASK

These tasks can only be done after you've
completed your MIT

☐ ....

☐ ....

ADDITIONAL TASKS & REMINDERS

List additional tasks and reminders for the day.

☐ ....

☐ ....

☐ ....

☐ ....

☐ ....

☐ ....

🖊 In Progress	▣ Completed
☒ Deleted	⇨ Deferred

6 ——————————

7 ——————————

8 ——————————

9 ——————————

10 ——————————

11 ——————————

12 ——————————

1 ——————————

2 ——————————

3 ——————————

4 ——————————

5 ——————————

6 ——————————

7 ——————————

NOTES / IDEAS

Write down any notes or ideas you have today. For future reference, index them on page 5.

SATURDAY / /

MOST IMPORTANT TASK

What can you accomplish today to meet your
weekly objective?

☐ ....

....

SECONDARY TASK

These tasks can only be done after you've
completed your MIT

☐ ....

☐ ....

ADDITIONAL TASKS & REMINDERS

List additional tasks and reminders for the day.

☐ ....

☐ ....

☐ ....

☐ ....

☐ ....

☐ ....

▨ In Progress	▩ Completed
⊠ Deleted	⇨ Deferred

6 —————————

7 ————————

8 ————————

9 ————————

10 ————————

11 ————————

12 ————————

1 ————————

2 ————————

3 ————————

4 ————————

5 ————————

6 ————————

7 ————————

NOTES / IDEAS

Write down any notes or ideas you have today. For future reference, index them on page 5.

SUNDAY   /   /

MOST IMPORTANT TASK

What can you accomplish today to meet your
weekly objective?

☐ ....

SECONDARY TASK

These tasks can only be done after you've
completed your MIT

☐ ....

☐ ....

ADDITIONAL TASKS & REMINDERS

List additional tasks and reminders for the day.

☐ ....

☐ ....

☐ ....

☐ ....

☐ ....

☐ ....

▨ In Progress   ▨ Completed

☒ Deleted   ⇨ Deferred

6 ——————————————————

7 ——————————————————

8 ——————————————————

9 ——————————————————

10 —————————————————

11 —————————————————

12 —————————————————

1 ——————————————————

2 ——————————————————

3 ——————————————————

4 ——————————————————

5 ——————————————————

6 ——————————————————

7 ——————————————————

NOTES / IDEAS

Write down any notes or ideas you have today. For future reference, index them on page 5.

WEEK 11 COMMITMENT

WEEKS LEFT IN QUARTER

`13` `12` `11` `10` `9` `8` `7` `6` `5` `4` `3` `2` `1`

Restate your goals each week to maintain your focus

PRIMARY GOAL

....

SECONDARY GOAL

....

TERTIARY GOAL

....

MUST-DELIVER TASK

What is the most relevant milestone in your Action Plan at the moment?
Towards achieving this milestone, what is the most important task you must finish this week?

☐ .... **A***

SECONDARY TASKS

List and prioritise secondary tasks using:

A = Must do this week

B = Good to do this week

C = Can do next week

☐ ....

☐ ....

☐ ....

☐ ....

☐ ....

☐ ....

Keep track of the progress you make on every task using these symbols:

▢ In Progress   ▢ Completed   ☒ Deleted   ⇨ Deferred

AFTER-ACTION REVIEW

Review your results after completing your work week by answering the following questions:

HOW FAR DID YOU GET?

Evaluate your progress and visualise it using the progress bars.

PRIMARY GOAL	20%	40%	60%	80%	
SECONDARY GOAL	20%	40%	60%	80%	
TERTIARY GOAL	20%	40%	60%	80%	

☐ In Progress   ☐ Completed

WHAT IS WORKING?

List the activities you've completed in the past few weeks that you should focus on more.

1. ....

2. ....

3. ....

WHAT DIDN'T WORK?

List the activities that need to be fixed, improved, or removed.

1. ....

2. ....

3. ....

WHAT DID YOU LEARN?

Take a minute to reflect on the biggest takeaway from this week.

....

WEEK 11

MONDAY	TUESDAY	WEDNESDAY
7		
8		
9		
10		
11		
12		
1		
2		
3		
4		
5		
6		
7		

THURSDAY	FRIDAY	SAT	SUN
7			
8			
9			
10			
11			
12			
1			
2			
3			
4			
5			
6			
7			

MONDAY   /   /

MOST IMPORTANT TASK

What can you accomplish today to meet your
weekly objective?

- [ ] ....

....

SECONDARY TASK

These tasks can only be done after you've
completed your MIT

- [ ] ....
- [ ] ....

ADDITIONAL TASKS & REMINDERS

List additional tasks and reminders for the day.

- [ ] ....
- [ ] ....
- [ ] ....
- [ ] ....
- [ ] ....
- [ ] ....

In Progress   Completed

Deleted   Deferred

6 ————————————————

7 ————————————————

8 ————————————————

9 ————————————————

10 ————————————————

11 ————————————————

12 ————————————————

1 ————————————————

2 ————————————————

3 ————————————————

4 ————————————————

5 ————————————————

6 ————————————————

7 ————————————————

NOTES / IDEAS

Write down any notes or ideas you have today. For future reference, index them on page 5.

TUESDAY   /   /

MOST IMPORTANT TASK

What can you accomplish today to meet your
weekly objective?

☐ ....

SECONDARY TASK

These tasks can only be done after you've
completed your MIT

☐ ....

☐ ....

ADDITIONAL TASKS & REMINDERS

List additional tasks and reminders for the day.

☐ ....

☐ ....

☐ ....

☐ ....

☐ ....

☐ ....

▨ In Progress   ▨ Completed

⊠ Deleted   ⇨ Deferred

6 ————————————

7 --------------------

8 --------------------

9 --------------------

10 --------------------

11 --------------------

12 --------------------

1 --------------------

2 --------------------

3 --------------------

4 --------------------

5 --------------------

6 --------------------

7 --------------------

NOTES / IDEAS

Write down any notes or ideas you have today. For future reference, index them on page 5.

WEDNESDAY   /   /

MOST IMPORTANT TASK

What can you accomplish today to meet your
weekly objective?

☐

SECONDARY TASK

These tasks can only be done after you've
completed your MIT

☐

☐

ADDITIONAL TASKS & REMINDERS

List additional tasks and reminders for the day.

☐

☐

☐

☐

☐

☐

◨ In Progress   ▨ Completed

☒ Deleted   ⊡⇨ Deferred

6

7

8

9

10

11

12

1

2

3

4

5

6

7

NOTES / IDEAS

Write down any notes or ideas you have today. For future reference, index them on page 5.

THURSDAY   /   /

MOST IMPORTANT TASK

What can you accomplish today to meet your
weekly objective?

☐ ....

SECONDARY TASK

These tasks can only be done after you've
completed your MIT

☐ ....

☐ ....

ADDITIONAL TASKS & REMINDERS

List additional tasks and reminders for the day.

☐ ....

☐ ....

☐ ....

☐ ....

☐ ....

☐ ....

▨ In Progress   ▦ Completed

⊠ Deleted   ⇨ Deferred

6 ——————————————

7 ——————————————

8 ——————————————

9 ——————————————

10 ——————————————

11 ——————————————

12 ——————————————

1 ——————————————

2 ——————————————

3 ——————————————

4 ——————————————

5 ——————————————

6 ——————————————

7 ——————————————

NOTES / IDEAS

Write down any notes or ideas you have today. For future reference, index them on page 5.

FRIDAY   /   /

MOST IMPORTANT TASK

What can you accomplish today to meet your
weekly objective?

☐ ....

....

SECONDARY TASK

These tasks can only be done after you've
completed your MIT

☐ ....

☐ ....

ADDITIONAL TASKS & REMINDERS

List additional tasks and reminders for the day.

☐ ....

☐ ....

☐ ....

☐ ....

☐ ....

☐ ....

▧ In Progress	▨ Completed
☒ Deleted	⇨ Deferred

6 ——————————————

7 ----------------------

8 ----------------------

9 ----------------------

10 ---------------------

11 ---------------------

12 ---------------------

1 ----------------------

2 ----------------------

3 ----------------------

4 ----------------------

5 ----------------------

6 ----------------------

7 ----------------------

NOTES / IDEAS

Write down any notes or ideas you have today. For future reference, index them on page 5.

. . . .

. . . .

. . . .

. . . .

. . . .

. . . .

. . . .

. . . .

. . . .

. . . .

. . . .

. . . .

. . . .

. . . .

. . . .

. . . .

. . . .

. . . .

. . . .

. . . .

. . . .

. . . .

. . . .

. . . .

. . . .

. . . .

. . . .

. . . .

SATURDAY / /

MOST IMPORTANT TASK

What can you accomplish today to meet your
weekly objective?

☐ ....

....

SECONDARY TASK

These tasks can only be done after you've
completed your MIT

☐ ....

☐ ....

ADDITIONAL TASKS & REMINDERS

List additional tasks and reminders for the day.

☐ ....

☐ ....

☐ ....

☐ ....

☐ ....

☐ ....

◩ In Progress	▨ Completed
⊠ Deleted	⇨ Deferred

6 ——————————————

7 ——————————————

8 ——————————————

9 ——————————————

10 ——————————————

11 ——————————————

12 ——————————————

1 ——————————————

2 ——————————————

3 ——————————————

4 ——————————————

5 ——————————————

6 ——————————————

7 ——————————————

NOTES / IDEAS

Write down any notes or ideas you have today. For future reference, index them on page 5.

SUNDAY   / /

MOST IMPORTANT TASK

What can you accomplish today to meet your weekly objective?

☐ ....

....

SECONDARY TASK

These tasks can only be done after you've completed your MIT

☐ ....

☐ ....

ADDITIONAL TASKS & REMINDERS

List additional tasks and reminders for the day.

☐ ....

☐ ....

☐ ....

☐ ....

☐ ....

☐ ....

▨ In Progress   ▨ Completed

▨ Deleted   ⇨ Deferred

6 ——————————

7 ——————————

8 ——————————

9 ——————————

10 ——————————

11 ——————————

12 ——————————

1 ——————————

2 ——————————

3 ——————————

4 ——————————

5 ——————————

6 ——————————

7 ——————————

NOTES / IDEAS

Write down any notes or ideas you have today. For future reference, index them on page 5.

WEEK 12 COMMITMENT

WEEKS LEFT IN QUARTER

`13` `12` `11` `10` `9` `8` `7` `6` `5` `4` `3` `2` `1`

Restate your goals each week to maintain your focus

PRIMARY GOAL

....

SECONDARY GOAL

....

TERTIARY GOAL

....

MUST-DELIVER TASK

What is the most relevant milestone in your Action Plan at the moment?
Towards achieving this milestone, what is the most important task you must finish this week?

☐ .... **A***

SECONDARY TASKS

List and prioritise secondary tasks using:

A = Must do this week

B = Good to do this week

C = Can do next week

☐ ....

☐ ....

☐ ....

☐ ....

☐ ....

☐ ....

Keep track of the progress you make on every task using these symbols:

▨ In Progress   ▦ Completed   ☒ Deleted   ⇨ Deferred

AFTER-ACTION REVIEW

Review your results after completing your work week by answering the following questions:

HOW FAR DID YOU GET?
Evaluate your progress and visualise it using the progress bars.

PRIMARY GOAL	20%	40%	60%	80%
SECONDARY GOAL	20%	40%	60%	80%
TERTIARY GOAL	20%	40%	60%	80%

In Progress   Completed

WHAT IS WORKING?
List the activities you've completed in the past few weeks that you should focus on more.

1. ....

2. ....

3. ....

WHAT DIDN'T WORK?
List the activities that need to be fixed, improved, or removed.

1. ....

2. ....

3. ....

WHAT DID YOU LEARN?
Take a minute to reflect on the biggest takeaway from this week.

....

WEEK 12

	MONDAY	TUESDAY	WEDNESDAY
7			
8			
9			
10			
11			
12			
1			
2			
3			
4			
5			
6			
7			

THURSDAY	FRIDAY	SAT	SUN
7			
8			
9			
10			
11			
12			
1			
2			
3			
4			
5			
6			
7			

MONDAY / /

MOST IMPORTANT TASK

What can you accomplish today to meet your weekly objective?

☐ ....

SECONDARY TASK

These tasks can only be done after you've completed your MIT

☐ ....

☐ ....

ADDITIONAL TASKS & REMINDERS

List additional tasks and reminders for the day.

☐ ....

☐ ....

☐ ....

☐ ....

☐ ....

☐ ....

◩ In Progress   ▨ Completed

⊠ Deleted   ⇨ Deferred

6

7

8

9

10

11

12

1

2

3

4

5

6

7

NOTES / IDEAS

Write down any notes or ideas you have today. For future reference, index them on page 5.

TUESDAY   /   /

MOST IMPORTANT TASK

What can you accomplish today to meet your weekly objective?

☐ ....

....

SECONDARY TASK

These tasks can only be done after you've completed your MIT

☐ ....

☐ ....

ADDITIONAL TASKS & REMINDERS

List additional tasks and reminders for the day.

☐ ....

☐ ....

☐ ....

☐ ....

☐ ....

☐ ....

◪ In Progress   ▦ Completed

☒ Deleted   ⇨ Deferred

6 ————————————

7 ————————————

8 ————————————

9 ————————————

10 ————————————

11 ————————————

12 ————————————

1 ————————————

2 ————————————

3 ————————————

4 ————————————

5 ————————————

6 ————————————

7 ————————————

NOTES / IDEAS

Write down any notes or ideas you have today. For future reference, index them on page 5.

WEDNESDAY / /

MOST IMPORTANT TASK

What can you accomplish today to meet your weekly objective?

☐ ....

....

SECONDARY TASK

These tasks can only be done after you've completed your MIT

☐ ....

☐ ....

ADDITIONAL TASKS & REMINDERS

List additional tasks and reminders for the day.

☐ ....

☐ ....

☐ ....

☐ ....

☐ ....

☐ ....

▨ In Progress   ▧ Completed

☒ Deleted   ⇨ Deferred

6 ————————————————

7 ————————————————

8 ————————————————

9 ————————————————

10 ———————————————

11 ———————————————

12 ———————————————

1 ————————————————

2 ————————————————

3 ————————————————

4 ————————————————

5 ————————————————

6 ————————————————

7 ————————————————

NOTES / IDEAS

Write down any notes or ideas you have today. For future reference, index them on page 5.

THURSDAY   /   /

MOST IMPORTANT TASK

What can you accomplish today to meet your
weekly objective?

☐ ....

SECONDARY TASK

These tasks can only be done after you've
completed your MIT

☐ ....

☐ ....

ADDITIONAL TASKS & REMINDERS

List additional tasks and reminders for the day.

☐ ....

☐ ....

☐ ....

☐ ....

☐ ....

☐ ....

☑ In Progress   ▨ Completed

☒ Deleted   ⇨ Deferred

6 ————————————————

7 ————————————————

8 ————————————————

9 ————————————————

10 ————————————————

11 ————————————————

12 ————————————————

1 ————————————————

2 ————————————————

3 ————————————————

4 ————————————————

5 ————————————————

6 ————————————————

7 ————————————————

NOTES / IDEAS

Write down any notes or ideas you have today. For future reference, index them on page 5.

FRIDAY / /

MOST IMPORTANT TASK

What can you accomplish today to meet your
weekly objective?

☐ ....

....

SECONDARY TASK

These tasks can only be done after you've
completed your MIT

☐ ....

☐ ....

ADDITIONAL TASKS & REMINDERS

List additional tasks and reminders for the day.

☐ ....

☐ ....

☐ ....

☐ ....

☐ ....

☐ ....

☑ In Progress   ▨ Completed

☒ Deleted   ⇨ Deferred

6 ———————————

7 ———————————

8 ———————————

9 ———————————

10 ———————————

11 ———————————

12 ———————————

1 ———————————

2 ———————————

3 ———————————

4 ———————————

5 ———————————

6 ———————————

7 ———————————

NOTES / IDEAS

Write down any notes or ideas you have today. For future reference, index them on page 5.

SATURDAY / /

MOST IMPORTANT TASK

What can you accomplish today to meet your
weekly objective?

☐ ....

SECONDARY TASK

These tasks can only be done after you've
completed your MIT

☐ ....

☐ ....

ADDITIONAL TASKS & REMINDERS

List additional tasks and reminders for the day.

☐ ....

☐ ....

☐ ....

☐ ....

☐ ....

☐ ....

▨ In Progress   ▨ Completed

☒ Deleted   ⇥ Deferred

6 ————————————

7 ————————————

8 ————————————

9 ————————————

10 ————————————

11 ————————————

12 ————————————

1 ————————————

2 ————————————

3 ————————————

4 ————————————

5 ————————————

6 ————————————

7 ————————————

NOTES / IDEAS

Write down any notes or ideas you have today. For future reference, index them on page 5.

SUNDAY   /   /

MOST IMPORTANT TASK

What can you accomplish today to meet your
weekly objective?

☐ ....

SECONDARY TASK

These tasks can only be done after you've
completed your MIT

☐ ....

☐ ....

ADDITIONAL TASKS & REMINDERS

List additional tasks and reminders for the day.

☐ ....

☐ ....

☐ ....

☐ ....

☐ ....

☐ ....

◪ In Progress   ▦ Completed
☒ Deleted   ⇨ Deferred

6 ————————————————

7 ————————————————

8 ————————————————

9 ————————————————

10 ————————————————

11 ————————————————

12 ————————————————

1 ————————————————

2 ————————————————

3 ————————————————

4 ————————————————

5 ————————————————

6 ————————————————

7 ————————————————

NOTES / IDEAS

Write down any notes or ideas you have today. For future reference, index them on page 5.

WEEK 13 COMMITMENT

`13` `12` `11` `10` `9` `8` `7` `6` `5` `4` `3` `2` `1`

Restate your goals each week to maintain your focus

PRIMARY GOAL

SECONDARY GOAL

TERTIARY GOAL

MUST-DELIVER TASK

What is the most relevant milestone in your Action Plan at the moment?
Towards achieving this milestone, what is the most important task you must finish this week?

☐ --- **A***

SECONDARY TASKS

List and prioritise secondary tasks using:

A = Must do this week

B = Good to do this week

C = Can do next week

☐ ---

☐ ---

☐ ---

☐ ---

☐ ---

☐ ---

Keep track of the progress you make on every task using these symbols:

◨ In Progress   ◨ Completed   ☒ Deleted   ⇨ Deferred

AFTER-ACTION REVIEW

Review your results after completing your work week by answering the following questions:

HOW FAR DID YOU GET?
Evaluate your progress and visualise it using the progress bars.

PRIMARY GOAL	20%	40%	60%	80%
SECONDARY GOAL	20%	40%	60%	80%
TERTIARY GOAL	20%	40%	60%	80%

☐ In Progress   ☐ Completed

WHAT IS WORKING?
List the activities you've completed in the past few weeks that you should focus on more.

1. ....
2. ....
3. ....

WHAT DIDN'T WORK?
List the activities that need to be fixed, improved, or removed.

1. ....
2. ....
3. ....

WHAT DID YOU LEARN?
Take a minute to reflect on the biggest takeaway from this week.

....

WEEK 13

MONDAY	TUESDAY	WEDNESDAY
7		
8		
9		
10		
11		
12		
1		
2		
3		
4		
5		
6		
7		

THURSDAY	FRIDAY	SAT	SUN
7			
8			
9			
10			
11			
12			
1			
2			
3			
4			
5			
6			
7			

MONDAY / /

MOST IMPORTANT TASK

What can you accomplish today to meet your
weekly objective?

☐ ....

SECONDARY TASK

These tasks can only be done after you've
completed your MIT

☐ ....

☐ ....

ADDITIONAL TASKS & REMINDERS

List additional tasks and reminders for the day.

☐ ....

☐ ....

☐ ....

☐ ....

☐ ....

☐ ....

▨ In Progress   ▨ Completed

⊠ Deleted   ⇨ Deferred

6 ——————————

7 ——————————

8 ——————————

9 ——————————

10 ——————————

11 ——————————

12 ——————————

1 ——————————

2 ——————————

3 ——————————

4 ——————————

5 ——————————

6 ——————————

7 ——————————

NOTES / IDEAS

Write down any notes or ideas you have today. For future reference, index them on page 5.

TUESDAY   /   /

MOST IMPORTANT TASK

What can you accomplish today to meet your
weekly objective?

☐ ....

....

SECONDARY TASK

These tasks can only be done after you've
completed your MIT

☐ ....

☐ ....

ADDITIONAL TASKS & REMINDERS

List additional tasks and reminders for the day.

☐ ....

☐ ....

☐ ....

☐ ....

☐ ....

☐ ....

6 ————————————————

7 ————————————————

8 ————————————————

9 ————————————————

10 ————————————————

11 ————————————————

12 ————————————————

1 ————————————————

2 ————————————————

3 ————————————————

4 ————————————————

5 ————————————————

6 ————————————————

7 ————————————————

| ▨ In Progress | ▨ Completed |
| ☒ Deleted | ⇨ Deferred |

NOTES / IDEAS

Write down any notes or ideas you have today. For future reference, index them on page 5.

WEDNESDAY   /   /

MOST IMPORTANT TASK

What can you accomplish today to meet your weekly objective?

☐ ....

SECONDARY TASK

These tasks can only be done after you've completed your MIT

☐ ....

☐ ....

ADDITIONAL TASKS & REMINDERS

List additional tasks and reminders for the day.

☐ ....

☐ ....

☐ ....

☐ ....

☐ ....

☐ ....

▧ In Progress   ▨ Completed

⊠ Deleted   ⇨ Deferred

6 —————————————

7 ——————————————

8 ——————————————

9 ——————————————

10 —————————————

11 ——————————————

12 ——————————————

1 ——————————————

2 ——————————————

3 ——————————————

4 ——————————————

5 ——————————————

6 ——————————————

7 ——————————————

NOTES / IDEAS

Write down any notes or ideas you have today. For future reference, index them on page 5.

THURSDAY   /   /

MOST IMPORTANT TASK

What can you accomplish today to meet your
weekly objective?

SECONDARY TASK

These tasks can only be done after you've
completed your MIT

ADDITIONAL TASKS & REMINDERS

List additional tasks and reminders for the day.

In Progress   Completed

Deleted   Deferred

6

7

8

9

10

11

12

1

2

3

4

5

6

7

NOTES / IDEAS

Write down any notes or ideas you have today. For future reference, index them on page 5.

FRIDAY / /

MOST IMPORTANT TASK

What can you accomplish today to meet your
weekly objective?

☐ ....

....

SECONDARY TASK

These tasks can only be done after you've
completed your MIT

☐ ....

☐ ....

ADDITIONAL TASKS & REMINDERS

List additional tasks and reminders for the day.

☐ ....

☐ ....

☐ ....

☐ ....

☐ ....

☐ ....

▨ In Progress	▨ Completed
☒ Deleted	⇨ Deferred

6 ——————————————

7 ——————————————

8 ——————————————

9 ——————————————

10 ——————————————

11 ——————————————

12 ——————————————

1 ——————————————

2 ——————————————

3 ——————————————

4 ——————————————

5 ——————————————

6 ——————————————

7 ——————————————

NOTES / IDEAS

Write down any notes or ideas you have today. For future reference, index them on page 5.

SATURDAY / /

MOST IMPORTANT TASK

What can you accomplish today to meet your
weekly objective?

☐ ....

SECONDARY TASK

These tasks can only be done after you've
completed your MIT

☐ ....

☐ ....

ADDITIONAL TASKS & REMINDERS

List additional tasks and reminders for the day.

☐ ....

☐ ....

☐ ....

☐ ....

☐ ....

☐ ....

▨ In Progress   ▨ Completed

⊠ Deleted   ⇨ Deferred

6 ————————————

7 ————————————

8 ————————————

9 ————————————

10 ———————————

11 ———————————

12 ———————————

1 ————————————

2 ————————————

3 ————————————

4 ————————————

5 ————————————

6 ————————————

7 ————————————

NOTES / IDEAS

Write down any notes or ideas you have today. For future reference, index them on page 5.

SUNDAY   /   /

MOST IMPORTANT TASK

What can you accomplish today to meet your
weekly objective?

SECONDARY TASK

These tasks can only be done after you've
completed your MIT

ADDITIONAL TASKS & REMINDERS

List additional tasks and reminders for the day.

6

7

8

9

10

11

12

1

2

3

4

5

6

7

In Progress   Completed

Deleted   Deferred

NOTES / IDEAS

Write down any notes or ideas you have today. For future reference, index them on page 5.

NOTES

Write down any notes or ideas you have today. For future reference, index them on page 5.

NOTE PAGE 2

NOTE PAGE 16

eVOLUTIon
BUSINESS CONSULTING

Alan Short

FOUNDER & LEAD COACH

alan.short@evolutionbusiness.com.au

USE THE QR CODE TO DOWNLOAD
AND SAVE ALAN'S CONTACT DETAILS